The Second Vatican Council

The Second Vatican Council

Celebrating its Achievements and the Future

Edited by
Gavin D'Costa
and
Emma Jane Harris

B L O O M S B U R Y
LONDON • NEW DELHI • NEW YORK • SYDNEY

Bloomsbury T&T Clark

An imprint of Bloomsbury Publishing Plc

50 Bedford Square
London
WC1B 3DP
UK

1385 Broadway
New York
NY 10018
USA

www.bloomsbury.com

Bloomsbury is a registered trade mark of Bloomsbury Publishing Plc

First published 2013

British Library Cataloguing-in-Publication Data
A catalogue record for this book is available from the British Library.

ISBN: HB: 978-0-567-24300-3
PB: 978-0-567-17911-1
ePDF: 978-0-56732-241-8
epub: 978-0-56705-163-9

Library of Congress Cataloging-in-Publication Data
The Second Vatican Council/Gavin D'Costa and Emma Harris p.cm
Includes bibliographic references and index.
ISBN 978-0-567-24300-3 (hardcover) – ISBN 978-0-567-17911-1 (pbk.)

Typeset by Deanta Global Publishing Services, Chennai, India
Printed and bound in Great Britain

Dedicated to our mothers
Lucy D'Costa
and
Ann-Marie Harris

CONTENTS

CONTRIBUTORS

Reverend Matthew L. Lamb

Revd Matthew L. Lamb was professor of Theology at Ave Maria University, Naples, Florida, S.T.L., Dr Theol. and priest of the Archdiocese of Milwaukee. His books include *Eternity, Time and the Life of Wisdom; Thomas Aquinas's Commentary on Ephesians; History, Method and Theology; Solidarity with Victims.* He edited *Creativity and Method: Essays in Honor of Bernard Lonergan; Catholicism and America: Challenges and Prospects; Vatican II: Renewal Within Tradition.* He has published over –145 articles dealing with St Augustine, St Thomas Aquinas, theological method, political theology, modernism, communication theory and the writings of Popes John Paul II and Benedict XVI.

Godfried Cardinal Danneels

Godfried Cardinal Danneels was the Metropolitan Archbishop of Mechelen-Brussels from 1983 to 2010 and chairman of the Belgian episcopal conference between 1979 and 2010. He has studied at the University of Leuven and the Pontifical Gregorian University in Rome, and was actively involved in writing the Second Vatican Council document *Sacrosanctum Concilium.* Major publications include: *Words of Life* (1991) and *Messengers of Joy: How Important is Priesthood Today?* (1995) and *The Road to Bethlehem: The Quest for Happiness* (1995).

Bishop Declan Lang

Bishop Declan Lang is Bishop of Clifton. Within the Bishops' Conference of England and Wales he is chair of the Department of International Affairs. He sits on the Mixed Commission for

Bishops and Major Religious Superiors and is a member of the Bishops' Conference Department of Christian Responsibility and Citizenship. He is one of the vice chairs of the National Catholic Safeguarding Commission and is also a Trustee of Missio – The Pontifical Missionary Societies.

Reverend Dr James Hanvey SJ

Rev Dr James Hanvey currently holds the LoSchiavo Chair in Catholic Social Thought, University of San Francisco. Previously he was head of the Theology Department and director of the Heythrop Institute for Religion, Ethics and Public Life at Heythrop College, University of London. He has written widely on a number of themes, especially on the Church's mission to contemporary culture and Ignatian Spirituality As of December 2013, Dr. Hanvey will be Master of Campion Hall, Oxford University.

Monsignor Timothy Menezes

Mgr Timothy Menezes is a priest of the Archdiocese of Birmingham and, since 2011, has been the Vicar General of the Diocese. He studied for the Priesthood at Oscott College in Birmingham and the Venerable English College in Rome, and studied liturgy at the Pontifical Liturgical Institute of St Anselm in Rome. In 2010, as Parish Priest of St Thomas More Parish in Coventry, he was appointed director of Liturgy for the Mass of Beatification of Cardinal John Henry Newman, celebrated by Pope Benedict XVI, at Cofton Park in Birmingham.

Professor Paul D. Murray

Paul D. Murray is professor of Systematic Theology in the Department of Theology and Religion at Durham University, where he is also director of the Centre for Catholic Studies. He serves on the third phase of work of the Anglican-Roman Catholic International Commission (ARCIC III) and is a Consultor to the Pontifical Council for Justice and Peace. He is editor of *Receptive Ecumenism and the Call to Catholic Learning: Exploring a Way for Contemporary Ecumenism* (2008), and co-editor of *Ressourcement: A Movement for Renewal in Twentieth Century Catholic Theology* (2012).

Professor Gavin D'Costa

Gavin D'Costa is professor of Catholic Theology in the Department of Religion and Theology, University of Bristol. His recent publications include *Christianity and the World Religions* (2009), ed. *The Catholic Church and the World Religions* (2011) and forthcoming: *Vatican II: Hermeneutics and Other Religions* (Oxford University Press, 2014) and a collection of poems: *Making Nothing Happen* (Ashgate, 2013). His research interests are in Catholic theology and theology of religions.

Professor Tina Beattie

Tina Beattie is professor of Catholic Studies and director of the Digby Stuart Research Centre for Religion, Society and Human Flourishing at the University of Roehampton, London. She writes and lectures on Mary and the Church, theology and art, theology and gender, and human rights and women's rights. Her latest book is *Theology after Postmodernity: Divinising the Void* (Oxford and New York: Oxford University Press, 2013 – forthcoming). Other publications include *God's Mother, Eve's Advocate: A Marian Narrative of Women's Salvation* (London and New York: Continuum, 2002) and *The New Atheists: The Twilight of Reason and the War on Religion* (London: Darton, Longman & Todd, 2007; Maryknoll NY: Orbis Books, 2008).

Doctor Ralph Martin

Ralph Martin is the director of Graduate Theology Programs in the New Evangelisation at Sacred Heart Major Seminary in the Archdiocese of Detroit. He is also the president of Renewal Ministries, a Catholic apostolate devoted to renewal and evangelization. His most recent books are *The Fulfillment of All Desire: A Guidebook for the Journey to God Based on the Wisdom of the Saints* and *Will Many Be Saved? What Vatican II Actually Teaches and Its Implications for the New Evangelization*. He has been appointed by Pope Benedict XVI as a Consultor to the Pontifical Council for the Promotion of the New Evangelization and served as a *peritus* at the recently concluded Synod of Bishops on the New Evangelization.

INTRODUCTION

The Second Vatican Council (1963–65) was a major Council in the history of the Roman Catholic Church. When Pope John XXIII opened the Council his intention was to teach and apply to the modern world the ancient wisdom of the Roman Catholic Church. In the complicated process of applying ancient doctrines to a modern context there were inevitably shifts of emphasis, sometimes bringing up neglected doctrines to address new questions or reformulating ancient doctrines so that they could be effective once more in the contemporary Church. Inevitably, after the Council there has been heated debate about the Council's meaning. We should not be surprised at this as historically Church Councils have often taken many years for their full impact to be felt, and in some instances, Councils have been forgotten within a few years and rarely referred to. The ways of the Holy Spirit are not always clear to men and women. But being forgotten or not referred to was not going to be the case with the Second Vatican Council, precisely because it spoke to the issues that still face the Roman Catholic Church some 50 years after: the importance of the liturgy as the single point of contact with many of the faithful; the meaning of revelation as revelation is the centre of Catholic faith; the search for holiness; the structures of the Church and the exercise of its teaching and juridical functions; and the Church's relationship with other Christians and the non-Christian world. That alone summarizes, all too briefly, the four Constitutions. The remaining Decrees and Declarations add detail and elaborate on these themes and together constitute a new epoch for Catholicism.

It was precisely because of this sometimes heated and bitter debate about the Council's meaning that Pope Benedict XVI declared that the year of faith that begins in 2012 and runs until November 2013 should be devoted to looking at the Council documents afresh. Going back to the original texts is always a good exercise in taking stock of what came after them. Of course, the Council was always more than texts. It was also the experience of the Catholic Church operating as a collegial body in a new fashion with voices from South America, Africa and India. What had been previously 'missionary' territories were now firmly part of the global and growing family. It was truly a world Council and after the first session, the European domination of the Council slowly faded away, although the Europeans and Americans outnumbered the rest. The legacy of the Council was contested almost immediately. The debate among Catholics could be classified, to crudely summarize, as taking up four possible positions. The first, often associated with so-called 'liberals', bemoans the fact that the radical changes brought about by the Council have been left behind – and sometimes, even reversed. The second, associated with 'traditionalists', mirrors the first. They bemoan the fact that the Council made too many radical changes, actually modifying and even sometimes overthrowing tradition. The third group, often called 'conservatives', argue that the Council taught in continuity with the Church's doctrines and anything 'radical' is a development, not a discontinuity, of doctrine. Finally, the fourth group are those Catholics who are not aware of the Council. Sadly the fourth group is quite large and that is certainly one audience that this book hopes to reach. But this collection is also aimed at the other three groups above. It represents writers from the first and the third groups outlined above and we think this is what gives this collection particular value. By bringing together this catholic diversity we want to indicate that the Council belongs to all Roman Catholics and more widely is part of the patrimony for all Christians.

Many of the chapters that follow began life as a series of lectures given under the auspices of the Clifton Diocese in Bristol, England. To this end particular thanks must go to Bishop Declan Lang and especially to Father Christopher Whitehead, the priest who made sure everything worked so smoothly and undertook so many tasks with grace and humour. But some of the chapters were also commissioned specifically for this volume, to give both an American and Anglo-Saxon perspective on the legacy and value of the Council. One of the unique aspects of this collection is the mixture of academics and pastoral teachers who came together to reflect on the legacy of the Council – and we have sought to preserve the differences in style and focus, given the differing backgrounds of our speakers/writers. In this way we are hopeful that they address both theologians and the layperson who is keen to find out more about the Council and its legacy. Each chapter is designed to help raise two questions: what did the Council teach about a certain issue; and what aspects of those issues are still with us and still in need of further exploration? This is both a critical and constructive task that brings together historical memory alongside the demands and questions from contemporary practice.

The area of coverage is understandably limited in a single volume such as this, but perhaps no apologies are needed in so much as these areas were isolated as the most pressing and significant for the contemporary Church. If the reader, Roman Catholic, Christian, Hindu, Jew or Buddhist, secular or atheist can find something of interest in this collection, then our purpose will be served. If that same reader is called into question by the claims of the Council, then the purpose of the Council and the gospel will be served.

It may help the reader to have an overview of the essays that make up this volume. Father Mathew Lamb opens the collection by dealing with the effect of the mass media on the Council and its reception. Charting how the Council was viewed through the world's media at the time, and how this led to certain conciliar misreadings, he distinguishes the 'real Council' from the 'virtual Council'. It is often the case that the latter has determined polarizations and has been ultimately harmful in the realization of the documents in the life of the Church. Godfried Cardinal Danneels provides us with an interesting introduction to the Council, placing the major themes in their respective theological contexts and then moving on to discuss the style and language of the documents which reflect the complex but clear voice of the Council. He emphasizes the importance of the continuation of Vatican II's message into the future and suggests practical measures which the Church can make in order to ensure this. Both these opening essays are useful orientation to the Council as a whole. The following chapters deal with specific aspects of the Council, before moving finally to an interactive overview.

Bishop Declan Lang, through a lively mix of personal reflections and a heartfelt look at the spiritual meaning of the documents, draws our attention to revelation. Considering *Dei Verbum* in particular, Bishop Lang shows us that the disclosure of the Word of God, for the Council, is not a singular or historic event but one which carries on into our futures and thus determines the way in which we relate to the world and to God. Moving onto the theme of mission, Revd Dr James Hanvey brings to the fore the Council's anthropological vision which connects *Lumen Gentium* to *Gaudium et Spes*. He offers an ambitious but self-critical examination which argues that we have now reached a new moment of reception and assimilation of the Council's work and that we are best placed to return to the documents for closer study, particularly in regard to how the Church can practically work out its soteriological dynamic – a key part of its mission of service to the world.

Monsignor Timothy Menezes takes a sensitively instructive approach to liturgy and church music. He discusses what the 'full, conscious and active participation' in *Sacrosanctum Concilium* means, in real terms, to the various 'types' of churchgoer. He uses, as example, certain situations which draw out the practical and perhaps sometimes unexpected tensions which arise in reading the document. Turning to the Roman Catholic Church's relationship with other Christian churches, Paul D. Murray examines the sometimes polarized but clearly existent difference between pre-conciliar and post-conciliar teachings on ecumenism. He reviews post-conciliar developments and addresses the issues which have followed the substantive change of teaching made in the Council documents *Lumen Gentium* and *Unitatis Redintegratio*, in particular.

Gavin D'Costa turns to the wider ecumenism and leads us into a deeper reading of the Council documents with a view to determining their stance on the non-Christian religions, with particular attention to Judaism and Islam. He approaches this from a 'liberal conservative' position and focuses on how the Council taught in continuity with Church tradition, as well as taking radical and positive steps forward in relation to the Jews and Muslims. He discusses how best to restore a proper balance in Catholic attitudes to other religions. Tina Beattie considers the treatment of Mary in *Lumen Gentium* and how this relates to overcoming the challenges which Marian devotion faces in the modern age. She locates Mary within the Catholic understanding of incarnation, salvation, Christology and ecclesiology, and looks to the Catholic theological concept of motherhood of the Church and the post-conciliar consequences of some of these teachings. Tackling the Church's methods in evangelization following the Council, Ralph Martin reviews the Church's pastoral strategy and suggests that now is the time for a 'rebalancing' of Christian message and its implementation in order to maximize conversion to the faith. Martin reiterates the fundamental urgency of preaching the Gospel and highlights failures in modern catechesis which may have resulted from a well-meaning down-playing of the theological justification for evangelization.

To conclude this collection and take a step back from the details of particular documents, Cardinal Danneels discusses, in an interview with Gavin D'Costa, his recollections of the Church at the time of the Council and the theological concerns then and now regarding topics dealt with in the documents. He reiterates his own personal vision for the continuation of the conciliar message into the future of the Church and world.

1

Vatican II after Fifty Years: The Virtual Council versus the Real Council

Fr Matthew L. Lamb

The fiftieth anniversary of the opening of the Second Vatican Council occasioned many reflections on the histories, the texts, the hermeneutics and the consequences of what has been termed the most important religious event in the twentieth century. Rather than discussing the superficial mass media framework on the Council, along with those who follow its division between 'conservative' and 'liberal' camps, the announced retirement of Pope Benedict XVI invites us to consider how well he has guided the Church's implementation of Vatican II. Pope Benedict was not surprised by the confusion so rampant after the Council. He called attention to the conflicts in interpretation that tend to follow significant ecumenical councils. He dramatized this in the case of the very first among such councils, Nicaea, by quoting St Basil the Great:

> The raucous shouting of those who through disagreement rise up against one another, the incomprehensible chatter, the confused din of uninterrupted clamoring, has now filled almost the whole of the Church, falsifying through excess or failure the right doctrine of the faith.[1]

---

[1] St. Basil, *De Spiritu Sancto*, XXX, 77; P.G. 32, 213. Quoted by Pope Benedict XVI in his address to the Roman Curia, 22 December 2005, 'Ad Romanam Curiam ob omnia natalicia' *Acta Apostolicae Sedis*, vol. XCVIII, 45.

While admitting that the post-conciliar period of Vatican II has not been so dramatic, Benedict XVI calls attention to contemporary difficulties in implementing the renewals and reforms called for by the Council. The genuine event of the Council was truncated to a struggle between liberals and conservatives, and the documents of the Council were misread within what Benedict XVI accurately terms a hermeneutics of rupture and discontinuity. The 'spirit' of the Council was severed from the texts promulgated by the Council. The texts are 'compromises' that contain, as Benedict XVI states, 'many old and ultimately useless things that had to be dragged along' in order to 'make room for the new'. This way of interpreting the Council, he asserts, found 'favor among the mass media' and in some sectors of modern theology.

In his address to the clergy of Rome on 14 February 2013, he forcefully put forward some parting reflections on the 'two councils'. This was a few days after announcing his resignation and he spoke without notes, and from his heart. Most of his talk centred on the important changes that were required if the redemptive truth of Catholic faith was to evangelize the modern world. He spoke of the role he played in the important impetus for reform that came from the northern European bishops, supported by Blessed John XXIII, in reformulating the agenda of the Council, setting aside the rather wooden schema provided by the curia. This was, he said, 'a revolutionary act' taken by the fathers in full responsibility for their pastoral duties. The Church would no longer simply contrast its teachings to the errors of the modern world, but would seek to show how what was of value in cultures could be improved and elevated by the teachings and practices of Catholic faith.

A first and fundamental priority is the true worship of the triune God in the liturgy of the sacraments and prayers of the church. So the first constitution promulgated was *Sacrosanctum Concilium*, as the fruit of liturgical and patristic theological studies after the World War I, reforming the worship of the church and encouraging strong sacramental participation; the minds and hearts of the faithful had to be centred on the great paschal mystery, the life, sufferings, death and resurrection of Jesus Christ redeeming the world created by the Word of God.

Then the church had again to be seen more strikingly as the 'Light of the Nations' (the constitution '*Lumen Gentium*'), and the unfinished work of Vatican I had to be strengthened and extended, linking the

Petrine primacy to the collegiality of the bishops; the teachings of Pius XII on the mystical body of Christ were enriched in the trinitarian ecclesiology of the council: 'the people of God-the Father are indeed the Body of Christ and the Temple of the Holy Spirit'. This was followed by the constitution on revelation, *Dei Verbum*, in which the importance of scripture was highlighted as the revealed Word of God proclaimed in the believing and worshiping church. A basic truth of the document on revelation is how the scriptures cannot be properly and fully understood except in the faith and worship of the church. There can be no disjunction between scripture and the handing on of the Word of God in the Catholic Church, carrying forward the visible and invisible missions of the Son and the Holy Spirit in the evangelizing mission of the Church.

The modern world at the end of the second millennium of Catholicism needed a response to the ecumenical movement seeking the reunification of the Church, as well as a response to the horrors of the Holocaust, and so the declarations on religious liberty (*Dignitatis Humanae*) and on the abiding covenant of God with the Jewish people (*Nostra Aetate*), as well as the wider dialogue among the world religions, sought to enlighten major concerns and hopes of so many peoples. These concerns and hopes were taken up in the final constitution of the Church and the Modern World (*Gaudium et Spes*). In all of this Pope Benedict speaks of the challenges and changes as true developments of the deep life of the Church's Catholic and Apostolic faith. But why the turmoil after the Council? He concludes his talk in ways that electrified the audience.

Permit me to quote at length:

I would now like to add another point: there was the Council of the fathers – the true Council – but there was also the Council of the media. It was almost a Council unto itself, and the world perceived the Council through these, through the media. Therefore the Council that immediately and efficiently arrived to the people was that of the media, not that of the fathers. And while the Council of the fathers was realized within the faith, and was a Council of the faith that seeks "intellectus," that seeks to understand itself and seeks to understand the signs of God at that moment, that seeks to respond to the challenge of God at that moment and to find in the Word of God the word for today and tomorrow, while the whole Council – as I have said – was moving within the faith, as "fides quaerens intellectum," the Council of the journalists was not realized, naturally, within the faith, but within the categories of today's media, meaning outside of the faith, with a different hermeneutic. It was a political hermeneutic. For the media, the Council was a political struggle, a power struggle between different currents in the Church. It was obvious that the media were taking sides with that part which seemed to them to have the most in common with their world. There were those who were seeking the decentralization of the Church, power for the bishops and then, through the expression "people of God," the power of the people, of the laity. There was this threefold question: the power of the pope, then transferred to the power of the bishops and to the power of all, popular sovereignty. Naturally, for them this was the side to approve of, to promulgate, to favor. And so also for the liturgy: the liturgy was not of interest as an act of faith, but as a matter where understandable things are done, a matter of community activity, a profane matter. And we know that there was a tendency, that was also founded historically, to say: sacrality is a pagan thing, perhaps even in the Old Testament, but in the New all that matters is that Christ died outside: that is, outside of the gates, meaning in the profane world. A sacrality therefore to be brought to an end, profanity of worship as well: worship is not worship but an act of the whole, of common participation, and thus also participation as activity. These translations, trivializations of the idea of the Council were virulent in the praxis of the application of liturgical reform; they were born in a vision of the Council outside of its proper key, that of faith. And thus also in the question of Scripture: Scripture is a book, historical, to be treated historically and nothing else, and so on. We know how this Council of the media was accessible to all. Therefore, this was the dominant, more efficient one, and has created so much calamity, so many problems, really so much misery: seminaries closed, convents closed, liturgy trivialized. . . . And the true Council had difficulty in becoming concrete, in realizing itself; the virtual Council was stronger than the real Council. [2]

---

[2] Quotation at: http://chiesa.espresso.repubblica.it/articolo/1350435?eng=y [accessed 12 March 2013].

Never before was an ecumenical council of the Roman Catholic Church so extensively covered and reported by the modern mass media as Vatican II (1962–65). The impact of this coverage was pervasive and profound in its portrayal of the Council in the ideological categories of 'liberal versus conservative'. The Council was dramatically reported as a liberal or progressive accommodation to modernity overcoming Catholicism's traditional conservative resistance to modernity. Foreign correspondents from 1962 to 1965 knew there were two international scenes that would guarantee their stories got top billing: the war in Vietnam and the Council in Rome. Journalists of the print and electronic media flocked to Rome with little or no expertise in Catholic theology. They depended upon popularized accounts of the Council deliberations and debates offered by periti and theologians with journalistic skills.[3] An American Redemptorist, Fr Francis Xavier Murphy, contributed much to the propagation of such 'conservative versus liberal' reporting on the Council debates in his widely read 'Letters from the Vatican' under the pen name of Xavier Rynne in the *New Yorker*.[4]

Pope Benedict has addressed repeatedly that the real council is one that emphasizes the underlying continuity in the ongoing changes and developments of the teachings and practices of the Church. Serious theological scholarship is needed, not simply the kind of superficial sound bites of the mass media. Pastors, theologians, catechists and all the faithful need to show how the 'real council' corrects the errors in the mass media's 'virtual council'. The reforms and renewals are in continuity with the principles of the Catholic faith and magisterial teachings. The reforms do initiate very real changes, but as the best works on Vatican II illustrate, they do not claim a 'rupture' with the principles underlying Catholic

---

[3]One theologian who was obliged by his superior to give daily reports for *La Croix*, Fr Antoine Wenger, A. A., called attention to the danger of ideological distortions in the mass media coverage: 'the journalist is in danger of writing merely ideological information, explaining everything categorically in terms of conservatives and progressives, integralists and modernists, doctrinal and pastoral, curia and pastors, Italians and non-Italians, etc.'. *Vatican Council II: The First Session*, trans. Robert J. Olsen (Westminster, MD: The Newman Press, 1966). See also Yves Congar, *Le Concile au Jour le Jour* (Paris: Editions du Cerf, 1963–66), 4 vols.

[4]These are collected in Xavier Rynne, *Vatican Council II: With A New Introduction by the Author* (New York: Orbis Books, 1968, 1999).

doctrine. The Pope himself illustrated this with reference to how Catholic martyrs illustrate a proper separation of Jesus Christ and any political regime. No Caesar, no political regime, can take the place of God. Christianity from its inception is trans-political. The Kingdom of God is beyond the bounds of earth and time.

The Magisterium of the Roman Catholic Church is properly understood within the theological and sapiential framework of Apostolicity. Irenaeus offers a powerful witness to the living faith handed on from one generation to the next down to our own day:

> Anyone who wishes to discern the truth may see in every church in the whole world the apostolic tradition clear and manifest. . . . This apostolic tradition has been brought down to us by a succession of bishops in the greatest, most ancient, and well known Church, founded by the two most glorious Apostles Peter and Paul at Rome. . . . For with this Church, because of its more effective leadership, all Churches must agree, that is to say, the faithful of all places, because in it the apostolic tradition has been always preserved . . .[5]

Without faith human reason cannot *theologically* understand the fundamental importance St Irenaeus attaches to the Apostolic tradition with its preaching, teaching, sanctifying and governing mission. The above quotation from St Irenaeus, born in the second century (probably between 140 AD and 160 AD), has the vividness of living personal witness, intensified no doubt by the martyrdom of his friend and mentor, Bishop Polycarp. St Irenaeus of Lyons knew the martyred Bishop Polycarp of Smyrna. He had reported to Irenaeus his conversations with the Apostle St John, 'eye-witness of the Word of Life', our Lord Jesus Christ. Jesus Christ as the Word of Life is not an abstraction for St Irenaeus – nor can he be for those who know him in the faith-filled worship of the Church. The very office of an apostle is defined by the initial 'follow me' that applies as well to all the successors of the apostles since the same Lord promised 'and behold, I am with you always until the end of the world'.[6]

---

[5]Irenaeus, *Adversus Haereses* III, 3, 1 and 3.
[6]Matthew 4:19; 9:9; 28:20; Mark 1:17; 2:14; Luke 5:27; 24:48; John 1:43; 17:18–21.

Early on Professor Joseph Ratzinger expressed this interpersonal character of Apostolic succession and tradition well:

> First and foremost, it is clear that *successio* and *traditio*, as they were first used, meant practically the same reality, and indeed were expressed by the same word, διαδοχη, which meant both tradition and succession. "Tradition" is never a simple, anonymous passing on of doctrine, but is personal, is the living Word, concretely realized in the faith. And "succession" is not a taking over of official powers, which then are at the disposal of their possessor, but is rather a dedication to the Word, an office of bearing witness to the treasure with which one has been entrusted. The office is superior to its holder, so that he is entirely overshadowed by that which he has received; he is, as it were – to adopt the image of Isaiah and John the Baptist – only a voice that renders the Word articulate in the world.[7]

This leads Professor Ratzinger to comment that it is not so much as readers of a book, but as hearers of the Word preached by the apostles and their successors that we must approach scripture in tradition:

> . . . if true apostolic succession is bound up with the word, it cannot be bound up merely with a book, but must, as the succession of the Word, be a succession of preachers, which in turn cannot exist without a "mission," i.e., a personal continuity reaching back to the apostles. . . . Apostolic succession is essentially the living presence of the Word in the person of witnesses. The unbroken continuity of witnesses follows from the nature of the Word as *auctoritas* and *viva vox*.[8]

The living Word requires faith. Any theology of Apostolicity and Magisterium can only be properly done with faith enlightening reason. If the light of faith is dimmed or extinguished, all that is left are texts as so many dead letters whose real truth is not grasped. There is a

---

[7]Joseph Ratzinger, 'Primacy, Episcopate, and Apostolic Succession', in Karl Rahner and Joseph Ratzinger (eds), *The Episcopate and the Primacy* (New York: Herder & Herder, 1962), pp. 46–7.
[8]Ibid., pp. 53–4.

profound inadequacy of purely social views of Apostolic succession as power and patriarchy. Instead a theological attention to the realities signified in the early fathers provides the following picture:

> The Church is the living presence of the divine Word. This presence is made concrete in those persons (the bishops) whose basic function is to hold fast to the Word, who are, then, the personal embodiment of "tradition" (paradosis – παράδοσις) and to this extent are in the apostolic line of "succession" (diadoch – διαδοχη). Conspicuous among the successors of the apostles is the line of the apostolic sees, which ultimately is concentrated in the See of Peter and Paul. This is the touchstone of all apostolic succession.[9]

This very cogent statement of the living presence of the divine Word in the Church mediated by Apostolic succession can be known and understood by theologians only when the light of faith enlightens their minds and hearts.

Some Catholic theologians have also kept the light of Catholic faith under a bushel in their writings on Apostolic, papal and episcopal authority. *Dominus Jesus* called attention to the importance of Catholic historical continuity:

> The Catholic faithful are required to profess that there is an historical continuity—rooted in the apostolic succession—between the Church founded by Christ and the Catholic Church: "This is the single Church of Christ . . . which our Savior, after his resurrection, entrusted to Peter's pastoral care (cf. Jn 21:17), commissioning him and the other Apostles to extend and rule her (cf. Mt 28:18ff.), erected for all ages as "the pillar and mainstay of the truth" (1 Tim 3:15).[10]

Today Catholic higher education has the great responsibility to recover and cultivate the wise traditions of philosophy and theology that are fundamental to Catholic intellectual life. Recent Popes have emphasized that this is for the sake of both the Church and the

---

[9]Joseph Ratzinger, 'Primacy, Episcopate, and Apostolic Succession', p. 59.
[10]The Declaration *Dominus Jesus* (on the Unicity and Salvific Universality of Jesus Christ and the Church) 6 August 2000, 16.

global cultures in need of moral and religious direction. The question of truth in matters moral and religious has to be raised within the context of the quest for wisdom, goodness and holiness. Truth cannot be consigned, as it was from the European Enlightenment onwards, as if it were an instrument of social or state dominative power. Both nature and history are ordered to ends inscribed in their very existence by their creator and redeemer. Both metaphysics and theology have suffered from the eclipse of wisdom in modern and postmodern cultures.

How many genuinely critical histories of theology are being written now? What passes for critical histories of religion and theology in modern secularist cultures are usually histories that are critical of (in the sense of negating) theology. They simply assume that what is really real is a secular horizon in which religion is at best a tribal prejudice or a private opinion, and at worst a neurotic delusion, or an ideology of oppression. In a secularist culture theology can become 'public' only at the expense of negating its claim to be reflecting upon divine realities. So-called critical histories are histories ignorant of these realities that are transcendently immanent in human history. This is precisely the danger of empiricist relativism and historicist nihilism against which Popes John Paul II and Benedict XVI have warned.[11]

Theologians must *know* the realities operative, the processes occurring, in living the moral life according to the teachings of the Catholic Church, in charity-informed faithful worship and prayer in the presence of our eucharistic risen Lord. One cannot do theology in the full sapiential and scholarly ('scientia') meaning of theology if one does not know in faith-enlightened reason the divinely revealed realities – without this, theology as a sapiential scholarly discipline ceases. Instead what results is a comparative textology that only recognizes as real what is admissible into a secularist horizon. It is as if the academy had lost any genuine knowledge of mathematics or science, and was limited to doing empirical and literary comparisons of mathematical and scientific texts.

Genuine theology is a way of discovery and a way of teaching that is informed with intellectual, moral, and theological virtues drawing upon both wisdom as achievement and wisdom as gift. As

---

[11]Pope John Paul II, *Fides et Ratio*, esp. pp. 80–108; Benedict XVI, *Regensburg Lecture* (12 September 2006).

gift, wisdom is a participation in the very wisdom of God, the Holy Spirit. Such wisdom is the love of God poured forth in our hearts by the Spirit who is given us (Rom. 5:5). It is this wisdom that guides the Church as it carries forward through history the missions of the Word and Spirit, cherishing the Word of the Father revealed in the Scriptures and worshipped in the liturgy. Such gifted wisdom from above evokes a cultivation of wisdom as a task to be achieved. Divine gifts neither deny nor denigrate human abilities. For these human capacities are themselves the gifts of God's creative love. So the theological virtues called forth, or evoked, the journey of acquiring the human intellectual excellence and moral virtues.

The bishops assembled for the Second Vatican Ecumenical Council – the 'real Council' – began each day's sessions with the Holy Sacrifice of the Mass in St Peter's Basilica. The reforms sought by the Council requires all Roman Catholics to deepen their lives of faith and learning, their sacramental participation in the divine liturgy as well as their many spiritual and corporeal works of mercy. In opening the Council John XXIII prayed that the 'sacred deposit of Christian doctrine should be guarded and taught more efficaciously' in order to respond with an intelligent and loving faith in Christ Jesus and his Church to the challenges facing both the Church and humanity at the end of the second millennium of Christianity.[12]

Theologians should avoid the temptations posed by the mass media sound bites of the 'virtual Council', forcing the Council into supposed oppositions of conservative versus liberal. This then enables them to manifest a superior ability to avoid the extremes they claim for others. As an example of this tendency, there is an essay by Fr John Conley, SJ.[13] The essay sets up imagined and facile contrasts between what he terms the Bologna versus Rome hermeneutical split. This split was personified in the books edited by Alberigo and the work of Archbishop Agostino Marchetto. The supposed 'duel', he writes, has American counterparts in a work by John O'Malley, SJ, and a book of commentaries on the texts of Vatican II edited by Matthew Levering and myself. Had he carefully read all the books he lists, he would have found that the arguments he gives for both continuity and real reform in the light of new situations are

---

[12]Pope John XXIII, *Opening Speech to the Council* (11 October 1962).
[13]Fr John Conley, SJ, 'Interpretating Vatican II: Beyond Continuity/Discontinuity', in *Fellowship of Catholic Scholars Quarterly*, 35, 2 (Summer 2012), pp. 14–18.

also given by Archbishop Marchetto and in many of the chapters in *Vatican II: Renewal Within Tradition*. Indeed, had he read the chapters on *Dignitatis Humanae* and *Nostra Aetate* in the latter book, he would have found even more cogent presentations of the real Council's teachings on religious liberty.

Thankfully, and in conclusion, Archbishop Marchetto has given us a second volume of his scholarly reviews of the ongoing reflections and debates on Vatican II. The Vatican published his *Il Concilio Ecumenico Vaticano II: Per la sua corretta ermeneutica* in November 2011.[14] Similar to his earlier volume, Archbishop Marchetto illustrates the importance of avoiding simplistic contrasts of 'continuity' versus 'discontinuity', of 'conservative' versus 'liberal', so dear to the consumers and followers of the mass media.[15]

Only the type of serious scholarship exemplified by this work and those of other theologians dedicated to understanding Vatican II within the Catholic and Apostolic magisterium will promote the reform and renewal called for by the real Council. As Pope Benedict concluded so forcefully in his February 14th address:

. . . the real power of the Council was present and, little by little, is realizing itself more and more and becomes the true power that then is also true reform, true renewal of the Church. It seems to me that, fifty years after the Council, we see how this virtual Council is breaking up, is becoming lost, and the true Council is appearing with all of its spiritual power. And it is our task, precisely in this Year of Faith, beginning from this Year of Faith, to work in order that the true Council, with its power of the Holy Spirit, may be realized and that the Church may really be renewed. Let us hope that the Lord may help us. I, retired with my prayer, will always be with you, and together we will go forward with the Lord. In the certainty: the Lord triumphs![16]

---

[14]Agostino Marchetto, *Il Concilio Ecumenico Vaticano II: Per la sua correctta ermeneutica* (Vatican City: Libreria Editrice Vaticana, 2012).

[15]Archbishop Agostino Marchetto, *Il Concilio Ecumenico Vaticano II: Contrappuncto per la sua storia* (Vatican City: Libreria Editrice Vaticana, 2005), pp. 223–43; also 93–165. See review of the English translation by Kenneth Whitehead, *The Second Vatican Ecumenical Council: A Counterpoint for the History of the Council* (Chicago: University of Scranton Press, 2010) by Gavin D'Costa in *The Tablet* 9 June 2011 and the letters by D'Costa and Matthew Lamb in *The Tablet* on 25 June 2011.

[16]See reference in footnote 2, above.

2

The Ongoing Agenda:
A Council Unlike Any Other

Godfried Cardinal Danneels

I What happened?

Vatican II was a Council unlike any preceding one. Even though it stands in a long line of Councils, it was in many respects a new kind of Council. It began more than 50 years ago. The Council Fathers themselves have now, for the most part, passed on. Believers experienced it from the outside through the media excitement and optimistic atmosphere in which this great Church gathering took place. The content of the conciliar texts – though often barely read – seems to many Catholics quite normal rather than radical. Many changes that had circulated before the Council were confirmed at the Council and are now almost commonplace today. Many people now are hardly aware that the content was so new for many at that time. Young people only vaguely remember the event, if they know it at all. They have rarely, or perhaps never, read the texts.

Nevertheless, Vatican II's documents have shaped the life of the Church for the past half century. Sixteen documents in all, and in particular, the four constitutions (on liturgy, revelation, the Church and the Church and world), have directed the thinking and action of the ecclesial community. Other decrees, such as those on ecumenism and religious freedom, were the subject of long-conciliar discussions and have really inspired new ideas and praxis. Texts on media and education, however, are now barely usable.

To understand the originality of Vatican II it is indispensable to look at the Council and its documents in terms of the history and culture of the time. Vatican II has certainly shaped part of that history but the reverse is equally true – history and culture shaped Vatican II as well. Even though it is true that Vatican II is fully rooted in our Catholic tradition, it also launched a development and a deepening of that tradition, which here and there shows a discontinuity with past thinking and practices. Many have observed (like Karl Rahner, for instance) that the Council marked the end of the Constantinian period in Church history and that Vatican II as a Council ranks with Nicaea and Trent in establishing a genuinely new period of development.

The Council had been prepared years in advance. The seed was already in the field and sprouting when Pope John XXIII called for the Council. The rays of sunshine from the Council have brought growth and much fruit. Conciliar preparation was particularly apparent in the early liturgical movement, in biblical studies (modern exegetical studies), and a renewed focus on patristics. There was also the influence of Protestant theology and various new philosophies. In contrast with the previous Councils which had usually been devoted to a particular theme, Vatican II addressed a broad variety of problems. Many issues were discussed, such as the place of the organ in the Catholic liturgy, the continued value of Thomas Aquinas for theology, the relationship between Rome and local Bishops, sexuality and marriage, the Church–State relationship and much more.

Important themes

If one takes a general overview, it is true that the main theme of the Council has been the value, role and responsibility of the laity in the Church in all domains. Yet another very influential development was the introduction of the vernacular in the liturgy. That may seem like a small detail but it actually launched a great dynamic that impacted many other areas – the ability, for instance, to change things that for centuries had been seen as unchangeable. Vatican II demonstrated that what was always thought and practiced need not necessarily remain that way for eternity. Perhaps the introduction of the vernacular was the first application of Pope John XXIII's *aggiornamento*, his bringing the Church 'up to date'. A dynamic was set loose that far exceeded mere linguistic changes. Nothing seems to have had a greater impact than changing ancient liturgical traditions because changes in cult and ritual touch very deeply the hearts of believers.

Also of great importance was the repositioning of Scripture, tradition and the Magisterium as sources of revelation, and the integration of the new exegetical methods into the study of the Scriptures. *Nostra Aetate* – the document on the relationship with the Jews – achieved a satisfying and surprising consensus, despite a long and sharp discussion and the additional burden of political pressure. The text on religious freedom and the relationship between Church and state has no equal in previous Councils and papal documents. Entirely new was *Gaudium et Spes*, the conciliar document on the relationship between Church and world. The Church took a listening attitude and said that it wanted to help the world. It claimed to want to move away from the world-rejecting, negative, defensive and superior attitude that had prevailed prior to Vatican II.

Finally, there was also a clear trend away from the purely consultative role of the episcopate by pushing – in some areas – for deliberative participation. In principle, the question of collegiality received a firm consensus of support in the Council. But no practical and legal procedures for its operation were laid down, except in the form of periodic Roman synods which will be discussed later.

New thinking and a different speaking style

Particularly noteworthy, before the Council, was the growing importance of a new genre of papal documents – the encyclical. More and more it was the Pope only who spoke to the Church and became the great and universal teacher. The encyclicals assumed more authority. They seemed sometimes to be dogmatic (and perhaps infallible?) statements. The concentration of the magisterium seemed increasingly to be located in the hands of the papal magisterium. With the emphasis on papal authority, a strong bureaucracy immediately developed – the Curia, which functioned as the central Church authority. The 'Holy Office' was their symbolic and effective voice. This Office, later called the Congregation for the Doctrine of the Faith, was the direct voice of the Pope.

Yet increasingly – especially in the twentieth century – a new understanding of the Church as the 'People of God' began to develop. This was a more horizontal relational understanding rather than the earlier vertical authoritarian model of the Church. The Church as People of God meant the whole Church as People of God – a large *familia Dei,* all brothers and sisters. Along with this horizontal understanding came the importance and influence of the developing world, an understanding that stressed democracy and participation. But – especially in the then burgeoning Catholic Action movements – lay men and women seemed to be regarded mainly as the submissive and generous employees of the Bishops. Besides the hierarchical ministry, however, there was more talk about the charisma of the free gifts of the Spirit to all of the baptized, without distinction. Not only were the ordained ministers seen as the Church but *all* of the people who make up the Church. A new vocabulary developed: charisma, participation, partnership, dialogue, cooperation, friendship. This vocabulary is present everywhere in all Council documents and has found its proper place in contemporary Church language.

Up until that time, the language of ecclesiastical authority was primarily juridical and legislative. It was rational, conceptual, concise and clear-cut. Vatican II chose a more pastorally-oriented language which was less clear-cut, more suggestive, not determinant but rather calm and serenely dialogical. The documents speak invitingly, starting with what speaker and listener already have in common. The Council uses a sensitive and aesthetic style which says that its message is true, good and clean. The old language determined and imposed whereas the new language suggests and invites.

Finally, it appears that we are in a new era for the Church. After the Jewish-Christian Church came the church of Hellenism. Now is the time for a real-world Church: the transition from European to global, from Thomism and Scholasticism to an assimilation of the philosophical and cultural thinking and praxis of the twentieth century.

Pope John XXIII

Then came Pope John XXIII. He was not only the Pope who decided on the Council and announced it but was the major catalyst for the transition from old to new. A Pope with not only a new name, he was 'well-rounded', both physically and in character. He was spontaneous and spoke and thought with great freedom and a healthy dose of humour, he was a Pope who never took himself too seriously. The way he announced the Council to his substitute secretary of state was typical. A few months after the beginning of his pontificate, during a daily meeting, he said, '*Faccciamo un picollo concilio*' ('We will hold a small council'). In Pope John XXIII's eyes it could be started and finished in only a few months' time. Indeed, while this is an entertaining anecdote about an inexperienced Pope, it also resembles an inspiration of the Holy Spirit. 'Out of the mouths of children and little ones . . .' (Psalm 8:2).

The renewal movement had been launched, the famous *aggiornamento*. Later even non-Catholics would be invited as Council observers. Pope John XXIII would broaden the range of issues, a positive attitude in the face of the 'world' and he would approach the other Christian Churches and confessions with a broad ecumenical vision. He had of course been *nuncio* where the Eastern churches were predominantly located, and knew this pressing need.

It should certainly be said that even contemporary cultural winds were blowing in that direction. Openness and broadmindedness dominated the scene. Along with that came the great power of the media. Immediately all secrecy was broken: every discussion, painful confrontation and debate was found in every evening news report around the world. Thanks to this media, the conciliar events had major world impact. Some conciliar texts – such as that on the liturgy – had already been put into practice before the Council was at its end. The Council also reached out to many non-Catholics and focused on all people. *Aggiornamento* became an almost magical word, bringing the tradition up to date. Other changes were very new: ecumenism and the attitude towards the Jews, the relationship between Church and state and the issue of freedom of religion. Finally there was the 'resourcing' or as it is called *ressourcement*, returning to the great tradition and to that time before Christians went their separate ways. The whole atmosphere of the Council was summarized in the opening speech of Pope John XXIII with the words 'Gaudet Mater Ecclesia'.[1]

The spirit of Vatican II

The difference between Vatican II and previous Councils is also reflected in the literary genre of the documents. The previous Councils were mainly a type of court that decided and eliminated some things but also legitimized other things and expressed itself in legal terms. Right from the start, this model was not adopted by the Council Fathers of Vatican II. Vatican II chose a different literary genre and a different language. There were no short position papers or judgements, no sharp formulations of belief and discipline, and very little normative language. The teachings of previous Councils were expressed mainly in the canons (the Council of Trent, for example, had 325). These were usually short position statements that were dismissive and always had dissidents in mind. The vocabulary was purposefully threatening, punitive and intimidating.

Vatican II chose longer texts and calmer statements that recalled the panegyric style of the Church Fathers. They instil wonder and invite the reader's engagement. The ideal is proposed and enthusiasm is generated. It all fits together under the word 'pastoral', rather than dogmatic. Pastoral is a soft term: dialogical and inviting. It stresses the goal of common conversion. Characteristic is the absence of terms of threat, punishment and exclusion. The texts were written on a more horizontal plane representing the relationship between the People of God and the world. Horizontality springs also from the notion of the equality of all the baptized – the priesthood of believers, collegiality, reciprocity, cooperation and dialogue and the ministry of the peoples' authority.

What people often lose sight of is the great attention Vatican II paid to interiority, holiness and repentance.[2] The Church in the

---

[1] Pope John XXIII's *Opening Speech to the Council* on 11 October 1962. The Latin text can be found at: http://www.vatican.va/holy_father/john_xxiii/speeches/1962/documents/hf_j-xxiii_spe_19621011_opening-council_lt.html. The English translation can be found at: http://www.saint-mike.org/library/papal_library/johnxxiii/opening_speech_vaticanii.html [accessed 12 March 2013].

[2] For example, see the call to holiness of God's people in Chapter V of *Lumen Gentium*.

documents of Vatican II is presented as 'good, patient, and merciful' as Pope John XXIII had already stated in his opening speech to the Council.[3] These words characterize him and the whole Council.

The liturgy, *Sacrosanctum concilium*

The spirit of the Constitution on the Liturgy is clear. The baptized are not passive spectators in the liturgy but rather they take an active part in the liturgy and have their own role in the celebration – hence the term 'active participation' was born. The idea was not a new one and had been present in the liturgical movement which focused on active participation, both inwardly and outwardly. Already in the preliminary draft, presented to the Council by A. Bugnini, there was a clear formulation of the fundamental principles of liturgical reform. One could read in this presentation the fruits of decades of the pre-Vatican II liturgical movement, especially since the Congress of Malines in 1909 and the contribution of Lambert Beauduin. Liturgy was not primarily a matter of rubrics and regulations. It was a full-fledged discipline with a doctrinal basis. The main emphases of Bugnini's draft were deep respect for the great liturgical tradition and a solid foundation of the liturgical action on the data of faith and doctrine. Great importance was attached to liturgical formation, especially of the clergy, and on a stronger participation of the assembly celebrating the liturgical action. Liturgy was not purely a canonical textbook for the 'doing' of the celebrant, but the making present of Christ's paschal mystery in its fullness – passion, death, resurrection and ascension. Chapter VII of the subsequent Constitution would later become the key text for understanding Christ's broad presence in the liturgy, in the praying people, the person of the celebrant, the proclamation of the Word and the communal praying of the psalms. Finally and above all Christ is discovered in the Eucharistic bread and wine. It was the rediscovery of the patristic vision of the liturgy.

The deep divide between celebrant and celebrating community was closed. Liturgy was a relational happening between God, the priest and the people. Very soon, the vernacular was introduced everywhere. And so the tradition of the unchangeableness of liturgical practice and use was overcome. Changing the liturgical

---

[3]Pope John XXIII's *Opening Speech to the Council.*

language was the breakthrough for making changes in other areas too. Finally, Bishops and Bishops' conferences gained more decision-making power about the liturgy, although this decision-making authority was soon reduced to submitting changes for approval and not just informing the central authority in the Church.

Verbum Dei

The Constitution on Divine Revelation is perhaps the most important doctrinal document of the Council. It was intensely and heatedly discussed but finally accepted by a large consensus. *Verbum Dei* touches the main coordinates of our faith: scripture, tradition and magisterium. Right up to the eve of Vatican II one had the impression that the source of faith was consulting the magisterium. Furthermore, tradition seemed to almost stand above scripture. There were indeed dogmas of the faith – especially, recently, about Mary – that could not be found *literally* in the Scriptures. Indeed it is true that scripture originated in the lap of tradition.

Nevertheless, the Council decided that the magisterium had only a mediating function between scripture, tradition and the People of God. The teaching authority of the Church had to *pie audire* ('devoutly listen') to scripture and tradition, the first sources of revelation. This could not be accepted without considerable discussion. Cardinal Ottaviani had stressed that the Magisterium had to teach, create order, bring clarity and speak concisely and clearly. He felt that such speaking should take precedence over a pastoral approach because the Magisterium manages the deposit of faith. In addition, scripture is literally inspired and the Old Testament is a pure introduction to the New. The Vulgate was the inspired text. Vernacular translations may be given to believers for their own reading, but for the crucial interpretation one must look to the Magisterium. A minority group in the Council has not ceased trying to neutralize the work of the historical exegetes. However, in the end, the majority of the Council Fathers succeeded in taking matters into their own hands. Some saw exactly here the *grosze Wende*, the big turning point for Vatican II. *Verbum Dei,* which consumed so much time and discussion, is unfortunately barely read today. This Constitution is however a pillar for conciliar work and, from a doctrinal point of view, is the crown of Vatican II.

The church. *Lumen Gentium*

The Constitution on the Church paints an image of the Church that is new and emphasizes different accents than the thinking prior to Vatican II. It completes but also corrects what Vatican I said. Vatican I was a Council of the Pope and his primacy. *Lumen Gentium* provides the missing complementary piece for integral thinking about the Church. The revised order of the chapters is very well known.[4] What is less often noticed is the chapter about the holiness of the People of God (chapter V). Vatican II did not only focus on the structure of the Church but also the Church's soul and heart. This focus on the interiority of the Church is certainly a novelty in a Council document.

The discussion about *Lumen Gentium* was clearly influenced by the intervention of Bishop E. J. De Smedt – an intervention on behalf of the Committee on Unity. Not only the content of his words, but even more so, his conviction and rhetorical impact were most important. Here, removed for the first time, in a conciliar gathering space, were words such as: triumphalism, clericalism, juridicism, pyramid structure and episcopal and papal idolatry. There was intense debate about papal authority and the collegiality of the Bishops and about the Church that had too greatly copied secular institutions such as the *societas perfecta* with its paternalism when speaking and its supremacy and exclusiveness. There was too much exclusive insistence on the Roman Catholic Church as the only true Church. There developed a different attitude towards other faiths. The attitude held that dialogue should be focused more on the basis of what Christians have in common and to stress what unites rather them rather than what separates them.

Church and world. *Gaudium et Spes*

The Constitution on the Church and the World is a novelty in the history of Councils. Earlier, when this topic had been discussed, there was a spirit of defensiveness – the Church cannot and must not form a pact with the world. The world was then almost exclusively

---

[4]Not the hierarchical ministry coming first but the text on the People of God, followed by the bishops.

seen as the 'world' as represented in John's Gospel. But it is the same gospel, John's, which says 'God so loved the world, that he gave his only begotten Son, that whosoever believeth in him should not perish, but have everlasting life' (Jn 3:16). In this vein, Vatican II turns positively towards the world. The Church knows that the 'world' at his coming did not accept Jesus. So it takes a listening posture, as it must, which invites dialogue and is not immediately judgemental.

There have been, in the course of our history, two models for interpreting the 'world'. On the one hand, there is the Augustinian interpretation which mainly states that the world has rejected Christ. Therefore the world cannot be seen simply in a positive way because it must be saved. On the other hand there is the incarnational interpretation which emphasizes the fact that God loves the world. He sent His Son into the world for humankind to love and be loved by. This is also the main interpretation to be found in the Eastern fathers. Both interpretations are valid and acceptable, but what is not acceptable is holding absolutely one, while denying the other. It is clear that the vast majority of the Council Fathers, when they arrived, were rather distrustful towards the 'world'. However, over a few weeks this gradually changed into a more open and optimistic attitude. There remained a minority – privileged by the Bishops and Cardinals of the Curia – who suspected the majority of disloyalty and betrayal of the tradition.

The role of the two Popes and their impact on the Council was varied. Pope John XXIII intervened very little and then, only on procedural matters. Pope Paul VI was variable – sometimes dampening, sometimes affirmative. The latter, an intelligent and sensitive man, was cautiously open and sometimes anxious and fearful. Yet he decisively intervened at key points such as on the celibacy issue, the *nota praevia* to *Lumen Gentium* and on the birth control question.

A rich harvest

The harvest of Vatican II is impressive. Often people have forgotten what happened and how much was achieved in practice. So many things are now taken for granted that the faithful are not even aware that such a sensitive change was due to the Council. But if one would make a list of all the fruits of Vatican II, one would see how greatly the Council has changed and renewed the Church. Liturgy and rituals were thoroughly reformed. Eucharist is the main focus and Baptism is strongly emphasized as the foundation for the priesthood of the faithful and the fundamental equality of all. The Eucharist and all the sacraments have a vernacular service in all countries and the reading schedule for Scriptural texts has a two-or-three-year cycle. Scripture is called the 'soul of theology'. The Eucharistic prayers were expanded. Christ is presented as a servant and friend of all people. The Council underlines the dignity of every human person – there is a new arrangement in the hierarchy of the ends of marriage. The dignity and mission of the laity and co-responsibility are stressed, as is the ideal of the Bishop as a servant and shepherd. The ministry of the Church to the world, the role of the young Churches, the problem of a just war and nuclear armament are yet more issues addressed by the Council.

Furthermore, there is the new style and language of the Council – pastoral, positive and not legal or juridical. It is emotive and not commanding. This style is more than just a detail. It flows from a particular new way of thinking. The spirit of the Council is certainly more incarnational than Augustinian. The collegiality of the Bishops was confirmed; but there was no agreed-upon framework on how to achieve this. Once the Council closed, the trend towards greater centralization began again. Power shifted back to the centre and the contribution of the periphery – Bishops and people – was not always strongly supported from the centre.

II What next?

The ideas of the Council are known. But what about their implementation? Is there still work to be done after fifty years? It is clear that the double hermeneutics – Augustinian and incarnational – will continue to exist side by side because both have their truth. And the search for a balance between the two will never be completely resolved. With this paradox, the Church lives and moves on. The temperament of Church leaders and their people, too, will always play a vital role. The crucial question is – to what extent was Vatican II a break with the past or a deep-rooted continuity with the past? What is Tradition? To what extent is, for example, the work in Vatican II on ecumenism a deepening or a development of earlier thinking and speaking? The same can be asked of religious freedom. We must ask also: how are papal primacy (Vatican I) and the collegiality of the Bishops (Vatican II) to be thought about together, so as to be fully realized?

The liturgy

Without a doubt, the Constitution on the Liturgy is the best followed-up on and put into practice of all conciliar documents. The reform of the cult has had a profound impact on the lives of the baptized. Everywhere there was a positive reception of the liturgical reform. Yes, there were wild experiments in some countries, but even so the positive fruits of this conciliar text are evident everywhere. The liturgical books have been renewed and around the world there has been a general introduction of the vernacular. Attention to the Word of God has increased and contact with the Bible expanded more fully. Yet there remains much to do to make that Bible more accessible to the People of God. What is needed is more Bible study and greater familiarity with modern exegesis, but these inevitably raise new problems as well.

The language used for the liturgical texts and prayers is often not as good as it should be. It is not enough to merely translate texts into the vernacular. Liturgy demands more than the home, garden and kitchen language. Liturgical language is always something sacred and transcends popular language. For the mystery of our faith we need a loftier way of speaking than just the language of daily conversation. There are words that belong to the language of Christianity that deserve reverent and deep interpretation. It is also true that rites and rituals are present and practiced in all religions. Often today there is resistance to repetition of the same words and gestures. Moreover, such rituals are not always immediately understandable and may not be considered as immediately productive and efficient. But ritual is not utilitarian; the ritual is the goal in itself. The Eucharist, for example, is a meal but a cultic and sacrificial meal not intended to satisfy our physical hunger. Trivialization or omitting certain ritual aspects deprives the celebration of its reference to the underlying mystery. Besides, symbols are always meagre – just think of 'symbolic' punishment.

Furthermore, the active participation of which the liturgy document so often speaks has to be understood as an overall participation. It is not limited to the outer doings. It concerns, as well, the innermost part of the soul. The Bible talks to us of believing and praying with the heart and not merely with the mouth and lips. Silence is an essential component in this active participation, for it links the way from the outside to the inside. The language of the heart necessarily transcends the language of the mouth and lips.

Another challenge is to find a balance between Word and sacrament. The Council has returned the Word to its rightful place. But here and there, the care and great attention paid to the Word has led to an underestimation of the sacrament. In terms of its duration and the attention given to it, the Word service in the Eucharist is often celebrated at the expense of the table service. Balance is needed.

A similar problem is that of balance between horizontality and verticality. There is sometimes a danger that the Eucharist is reduced to just its simplistic meal dimension at the cost of the *sacrificial* meal dimension. Of this there are no more examples in our current culture. The celebration facing the people suggests firstly the local community and puts less focus on God. But the Eucharist is both. It is a convivial meal and an act of worship and sacrifice. Much depends on the attitude of the celebrant. Eye contact should be there for the celebrating community, but first to God.

The church

The Council has clearly stressed the equality of all the faithful by virtue of their baptism. But this equality cannot be regarded as a mere democratic, levelling equality. The People of God is very specific and it is a combination of hierarchy and people. There is diversity in all its equality. That is also something no longer part of our culture, where all our power comes from below – the people choose their representatives. In the Church, authority comes from God.

This relationship between hierarchy and people must also take on its juridical identity. This has been a problem throughout the course of history, with varied legal forms situated between centralization and various forms of democracy. A related problem is that of the relationship between papal primacy and the collegiality of the bishops. The search for the best resolution stretches throughout church history. Will there ever be a perfect and definitive legal framework for this problem? Or is it to be resolved through a kind of love relationship where the Pope loves the Bishops and vice versa? After all, love alone is the master of paradox.

Nevertheless, one can ask if a sort of privy Council of Bishops and Cardinals around the Pope would not be a fruitful way to proceed. Such a privy Council would have to be limited and regularly renewed. It would consist of representatives from all continents who would meet regularly with the Pope – as a consultative body – to discuss the main problems of the Church. It would be an active forum where views could be exchanged between the Pope and the Bishops and insights could be gathered to assist the Pope.

To give collegiality some legal shape, the Church has opted for periodic Roman synods which meet at regular times. They consist of elected members of the episcopates from around the world. The synods have their value, if only as a place where Bishops can meet with their brother Bishops drawn from the whole, global Church. Socially speaking, the synods are useful and they do promote an affective collegiality. But when it comes to an *effective* collegiality they are much less helpful. They lack a real debate culture. In technical conversational terms, the synods fall short. One could ask if it is really possible for some three hundred Bishops to really discuss and arrive at decisions – even if they are simply consultative. The interventions of the Bishops are now more often newsletters, which provide information on the situation in many Churches. They are informative and interesting but often have little or nothing to do with the actual theme of the synod itself. Thus they contribute little to the discussion.[5] After half a century, the synods are still in search of an efficient methodology. Yet they are still the only place where collegiality has any legal shape. Is it not time to think about the purely consultative status of the synods?

---

[5]However, we must not forget the special synod of 1985, where an assessment was made of the Council to mark its twenty-fifth anniversary. From that synod came the *communio* idea as a concept for thinking of the Church, which was a Patristic understanding. But the name is suggestive, even though it offers no sharp canonical outline for the design of collegiality.

The church and the world

Gaudium et Spes is a document that is necessarily time-bound because is asks: how is the Church connected to the world? The world has evolved and many new problems have arisen. This constitution needs updating to come to terms with postmodernities and complex forms of modernity. A completely new document is needed. Since the Council, our society and our culture have become much more pessimistic and anxious. Where is the *Weltfreudigkeit*, the joy of Vatican II? Today there is widespread unrest and great concern despite major scientific and technical progress. Despite its time-bound nature, the Council has stimulated a powerful impulse. In many places it has had a strong social impact, especially in Latin America. It is undeniable that the voices of the Church and Pope are carefully listened to when it comes to global issues.[6]

Vatican III

Occasionally the idea is put forward about the desirability or even the need for a Vatican III. There is indeed something to be said for this. Many new problems have arisen in the Church and the world on which the Church needs to take a firm position. Pope John XXIII spoke of a new Pentecostal Wind and of *aggiornamento*, but has there been a new, real dialogue with the world? Some could argue that there is a lack of collegiality and a trend towards more centralism in the Church today. Some ask: what is the meaning and reason for traditionalist tendencies in the Church and the return to the old liturgy? And why is it that we find groups that do not accept the decisions of Vatican II? On the other hand it could also be argued that the minority view of the Council persists and grows while the majority view of before loses its cohesion and influence. For some, on all sides of this debate, the only solution is a new Council.

---

[6]Especially noteworthy is an initiative led by Cardinal Gianfranco Ravasi. Cardinal Ravasi spoke of the need for a more profound dialogue with nonbelievers in a project that took the name of the 'Court of the Gentiles'. This project, conducted in several large cities, is completely in line with *Gaudium et Spes*. It shows a willingness by the Church to listen and to talk about contemporary culture and philosophy.

We cannot disagree that the world has changed. New elements have been added, for example, the spectacular flowering of evangelical churches, Christianity's new relationship with other religions, the shortage of priests, the paedophilia crisis and sexual abuse by religious figures, the growth of feminism, the profusion of new communication technologies and the fear for the very future of the planet itself.

Some problems that were handled in Vatican II and led to a theoretical consensus are still relevant. There is the relationship between the centre and the periphery, the collegiality of the Bishops and the legal form thereof, the possible creation of patriarchates, the deliberative nature of shared decision-making, administrative transparency, debates open to the public and so on. Indeed Vatican II faced its own problems as is inevitable for any Council.

Would a new Council truly be the best answer? Organizing a Council is a matter of complex logistics. For many Bishops, travel and accommodation would have to be financed by the Church. The world episcopate today is immense and comprises 5,000 Bishops (not to mention the many other experts and guests who would be needed for such a Council). How could one technically organize communication for such an assembly? Perhaps we could instead have continental synods. At present there is little enthusiasm, optimism or hope for a Council. Have we not become too fearful? A new Council would not be mainly a European Council as was still the case with Vatican II. During Vatican II, the input came mainly from Europe. Are people in other parts of the world ready to take on such a task today? Instead we should consider whether the full realization of the decisions of Vatican II is the actual 'Vatican III' that we need.

3

A Word for Life: Vatican II on Revelation

Bishop Declan Lang

Many of us, myself included, are children of the Second Vatican Council. Pope John XXIII called the Council in 1959. What were you doing in 1959 and where were you? Most of us were alive but some not even born. I was nine years old, still at primary school and the calling of the Second Vatican Council did not make a particularly deep impression on me at the time. In fact, I probably did not hear about it at all. But I did learn of the opening of the Council in 1962. John XXIII opened the Council and invited 2,908 bishops to attend. This Council was different in many ways from previous ones. For instance, it was the first Council that knew electric lights; it was the first Council that used typewriters. It was the first Council that was reported on throughout the world in magazines and in journals. And poignantly, it was the first Council where the majority of bishops were non-European. European bishops were still the largest group in number but, put together, the other bishops from all over the world outnumbered the Europeans. The diversity of the Council itself reflected the growing change in the Church. In addition, when John XXIII called the Council, he did so in recognition that we were living not only in a changing Church but also in a changing world.

John XXIII gave three reasons for calling the Council. The first was that through the Gospel the Church might be renewed. The hope was that the doors might be opened to allow the Spirit of God to renew the life of the Church and the life of the world, giving us fresh hope. Second, it was hoped that the Church, in its renewal, might respond to the changes taking place in the wider world. At this time the world was still recovering from the World War II. The effects of that war were very much at the forefront of peoples' minds, particularly the very visual horrors of the concentration camps and the Holocaust. But another type of war was already also in progress – the Cold War. Pope John wanted the Church to respond in a creative way to a world still suffering from the effects of the World War II and the fears of this newer Cold War. As he said at the first opening session, he wanted this Council to be a means of making peace with humanity. Third, John XXIII called the Council because he considered the disunity of the Church a scandal. This was not helping the Church in her mission as the sacrament of Christ to the world today. The scandal caused by the disunity of the Church may seem obvious to us now, but that has not always been the case. Indeed at that time, as Catholics, we were not permitted to go into non-Catholic churches.

John XXIII was in many ways prophetic in his leadership, calling Christians of different traditions to come together. For that reason he invited representatives from other Christian traditions to come to the Council. When it opened, John XXIII noted that the calling of this Council, unlike previous Councils, was not because the Church was in crisis or being attacked by enemies from outside or within. It was not called to confront serious attacks upon the doctrines or organizational integrity of the Church. It was not called to repeat ancient formulas or condemn dissidence or heretics. Its goal was to:

> eradicate the seeds of discord and promote peace and unity of all human kind. Insofar as it will attend to doctrine the Council is to keep in mind the distinction between the substance of doctrine and the ways in which doctrine is presented to the people of our day. To do this the Church must employ the best methods of research and be aware of modern trends in thought and philosophy. The Council will prepare the path towards that unity of mankind, which is required in order that the earthly city may be brought to resemblance of the heavenly city.

These were the great purposes of the Council and it was hoped that through the work of the Council changes in the life of the Church would happen. That change needed to be at a deep level. It was and is fundamentally a call to conversion and holiness.

In his reflections on the Second Vatican Council, Bishop Christopher Butler pointed out that the majority of bishops who attended the sessions of the council underwent a deep conversion. For Butler, that conversion happened because the bishops in attendance were *open* to the power of the Word of God and the power of the Holy Spirit changes people. That may have been unexpected because it was also pointed out that the majority of bishops of England and Wales went to Rome with little expectation. It was said by some that the bishops regarded it more as a reunion of the English College.

I think that the changes brought about by the Second Vatican Council and the depth of their meaning still need to be explored today. The Council was about the Kingdom of God, about the person of Christ. The opening paragraph of Dei Verbum, issued on 18 November 1965, states in the opening prologue:

Hearing the word of God with reverence and proclaiming it with faith, the sacred synod takes its direction from these words of St. John: "We announce to you the eternal life which dwelt with the Father and was made visible to us. What we have seen and heard we announce to you, so that you may have fellowship with us and our common fellowship be with the Father and His Son Jesus Christ" (1 Jn 1:2-3). (DV 1)

From the very beginning of this document the purpose of revelation is stated that God reveals God's self to us in order that there might be fellowship, that we might be in communion with God and with one another and that being in communion with God and with one another, we may be a people of faith, hope and love.

I think that it is important to remember that as we study *Dei Verbum* and the other documents of the Second Vatican Council, we are doing so to examine their theology in order that we might be more effectively a People of God – so that we might more effectively be a sacrament of Christ in our world today – so that we might be more truly in communion with God and with one another.

I spend a modest amount of my time travelling between Bristol and Paddington. While I am not in any sense a railway fanatic, I seem to have to go to London frequently to attend meetings. Something I do on a train, which you may or may not do yourself, is to look around and wonder who are these people, where are they going and why? I wonder what these people think of me, the vicar with his collar. What do they *actually* think of the Church and of God? How can we and how are we communicating the love of God, the presence of Christ and the power of the Holy Spirit to all of these people who are travelling between Bristol and Paddington on a particular day? These questions are tied up, of course, with the area of revelation. Does God reveal God's self to a few people or to everyone? If God reveals himself to everyone, how does God do this? How do we recognize the presence of God in the lives of people who may feel indifferent or even negatively towards the Church and how do we recognize the presence of God and God's revelation to people of other faiths? These were the questions the Church was forced ask in the sixteenth century with the discovery of the new world. Suddenly, there were new populations who had never heard of Christ. It was important to understand where these people stood in relation to God and where God stood in relation to them. As we presently look to *Dei Verbum*, we are not looking at a mere document but rather the way in which God relates to us and how we relate to God. Also, how we relate to the wider world and recognize God's presence in the world. As *Dei Verbum* points out, the God we believe in is a God who wants to reveal himself to each one of us, to the whole world and to the whole of creation. The God we believe in is not a small or a narrow God. The God that we believe in is the God who will challenge us in the small horizons of our lives even though we may feel in life that our horizons are broad. If we are truly open to the presence of the God of the universe, then the horizons of our lives and our minds will be challenged. The God that we believe in is a God who wants to communicate with us in order that we might know our true self and that we might know God. The God who reveals himself to us is revealed above all in the person of Jesus Christ, the Word of God become flesh, the Word of God revealing God's self in God's fullness to us and to the whole of humanity.

There is in a sense no new revelation after Christ but there is always something new in Christ for the Gospel is something that is ever old yet ever new. As we open ourselves to the person of Jesus Christ, the manifestation of the invisible God, we will find that our lives are enriched and that we deepen our understanding of ourselves and of others.

As *Dei Verbum* also points out and as *Verbum Domini* then further explains, using the prologue of Saint John, in the beginning was the Word and the Word was with God before the Word became flesh. We are reminded that the God we believe in is a God of communication within God's self. There is constant conversation between Father, Son and the Holy Spirit. We are made in the image and likeness of our God and so is everyone. Because of this, there is within the lives of every single person a mark of God. Sometimes it remains hidden from us and remains hidden from them, but there is in each person a seed of God. The image of God is not only seen in human beings but is also there in the whole of creation. Because all things are made through him and for him, we can say that everything in the whole of creation is an expression of God. In creation we come to know God, and so, that first revelation of God comes through the whole of creation. We are called to recognize and to treasure the whole world because there is the first place of the revelation of God. Creation is not for our exploitation.

Returning to *Dei Verbum*, we hear those well-known words that are used on Christmas Day from the letter to the Hebrews: 'In the past God spoke to our ancestors through the prophets at many times and in various ways' (Heb. 1:1). In 'various ways' God has spoken to our ancestors and through the scriptures and through what we call the Old Testament we hear the story of how God has chosen a people, how he has entered into their story, to become part of their story and how, consequently, they have become part of God's story. The people of the Old Testament, our ancestors in faith, have been called into a covenantal relationship with God. We see this with Adam, Noah, Abraham and Moses, for example. As the people enter more fully into that covenant they began to understand God more fully too. They found the horizons of their lives were changed. If they believed that God was the God of a few and God of the tribe, then they gradually began to realize that the God they believed in was the God of all people. It is that God who is part of their life; it is that God who gives them life and identity.

People lose their identity as they turn away from God, as they chose their own way rather than God's way. Throughout the Old

Testament we hear of prophets who call Israel back to the covenant, calling the people back to their foundational identity through obedience to God's law. The purpose of the law is the same purpose that John XXIII mentioned at the Second Vatican Council – to draw people into true relationships, into communion with God and with one another.

In the Old Testament we find a call to justice, love and witness. The prophet Micah asks the people, 'what does the Lord require of you but to do justly, to love mercy, and to walk humbly with your God?' (Micah 6:8). In the Old Testament there was a sense of the power of God's Word – *dabar*. The Word is not just a communication. It is something that not only communicates but does what it says, it *does* what it first communicates. In the Old Testament God does exactly what he says he will in a supreme case of 'doing what it says on the tin'. Through the Prophets He gives people hope of a new age – a messianic beginning. That new age is found in the Word of God who becomes flesh because 'though in various times God has spoken to us through the Prophets and in varied ways', such as through creation, 'in our own day', as both *Dei Verbum* and *Verbum Domini* point out, God has spoken to us through His Son.

What therefore should be our response? Again, *Dei Verbum* and *Verbum Domini* have the same answer to that question. One develops the other. In the midst of this revelation of God, which we find in Jesus Christ, our response is to be one of obedience, not perhaps a popular word, but obedience in the sense that we freely commit ourselves entirely to making our full submission of intellect and will to God who reveals himself to us. This is a call to discipleship, to be an obedient follower of the Lord. As we are doing so our model of obedience is Christ himself. Christ, who though he was divine, stripped himself of glory and became humble and became like one of us. In giving his life on the cross he received a name above all names. Obedience brings us an understanding of the Gospel and draws us into a relationship that is life giving – the relationship of freedom. For as Jesus says 'I have come that they may have life, and have it abundantly' (Jn 10:10). To that life, Jesus invites his disciples. But he also commissions them, as he returns to the Father, and tells them to go out to the whole world and proclaim the good news.

This reminds us that revelation is not a historical story. The Word of God is proclaimed for our day and in every day, so that our relationship with the Lord may be a living one, may be a personal encounter and not just a past memory. To those first disciples is entrusted the Word of God. Those disciples are called to proclaim a message which is not their own but that of Christ. They are sent as apostles in the name of Christ – the word apostle meaning 'sent'. They are called to preach and live the Gospel and to choose successors who will carry on the office of teachers of the Word and guarantors of the story. Those successors we call Bishops.

The preaching of the Church is to enable Christ to live with us today and to draw all people into a personal encounter with the Lord. Some of those first disciples and early Christian communities put the proclaimed Word of God into writing. This is how we have the beginnings of the sacred scriptures of the New Testament. These scriptures are also the Word of God because they, like that which is preached, are inspired by the Holy Spirit. The New Testament – sacred scriptures of the new covenant – is related to the scriptures of the Old Testament – the old covenant. The Old Testament is a prophecy of the new and the best commentary on the Old Testament, of course, is the New Testament.

One of the great changes of the Second Vatican Council was the rediscovery of the Word of God and the importance the scriptures have in the life of the Church – in liturgy, prayer and catechesis. To go back to when I was in primary school, one of the requirements when I went into the senior school was to have a Bible. I discovered it was almost impossible to buy a Catholic version of the scriptures. What could be acquired were books on Bible stories but not the Bible itself. Eventually, after much searching, I managed to find a Douay-Rheims version. As mentioned, one of the great gifts that *Dei Verbum* has given to the Church is to rediscover the Word of God and to bring it into the centre of the Church's life. The Word of God is inspired by the Holy Spirit because the writers of the sacred scriptures have been given an insight into the life of Christ and his teachings and the Holy Spirit has used their talents and their gifts to communicate the good news.

At the time of the Reformation, one of the issues was the tension between scripture and tradition. If you proclaimed 'Sola Scriptura', you were a Protestant. Catholics believed in tradition and the scriptures. That is putting it very crudely but in reality this crude description was how it was for a number of people. *Dei Verbum* shows that scripture and tradition are not two things opposing one another but two forces feeding one another. They are both the deposit of God's Word. Tradition, in the Catholic understanding, is the way in which the Church has interpreted the scriptures over the centuries. Both scripture and tradition are inspired by the Holy Spirit and are not in opposition to one another.

Dei Verbum reminds us that we need to understand the scriptures as proclaimers and as listeners to the Word of God. We have a responsibility to understand what we are proclaiming and what we are listening to. We need to understand the different types of literature that form the scriptures of the Old and New Testament. We need to understand the mind-set of the people who wrote the scriptures in the first place in order that we do not misinterpret what they have written. We need to know the historical context within which the scriptures were written and each, exact situation to which they are responding. What is the truth that the writers are trying to uphold? What is the truth that they considered to be under attack? We need to remember that the truth of scripture does not lie within one book or in one verse but within the whole body of the work.

Dei Verbum reminds us that we have an obligation to those to whom we proclaim and teach the Word of God. This obligation is especially a responsibility for the clergy. The clergy need to have a deep knowledge of the scriptures so that what they preach makes sense to people and feeds them with truth. *Verbum Domini* declares that the Bible was written by the People of God for the People of God under the inspiration of the Holy Spirit. Only in this communion with the People of God can we truly enter as a 'we' into the heart of truth that God wishes to convey to us.

Verbum Dei and *Verbum Domini* remind us that the scriptures can be used for personal prayer and that they should be the basis of our everyday prayer. However, the scriptures are there for the Church and are to be read, listened to and celebrated within the context of the whole body of Christ. That is why they should be at the heart not only of our Eucharistic celebrations but of every sacramental celebration. *Verbum Domini* teaches us that when nowadays a number of ecclesial communities are unable to celebrate the Eucharist on a Sunday, they should still feel an obligation to gather, to listen and to celebrate the Word of God because it is ever alive and active.

To return to the people of the train tomorrow morning. I do not know who they are or where they are going. They may be nearer to God than I am. All we can know is that God wishes to communicate to us all and that God wishes to reveal himself to all of us. That revelation is a revelation of God's love because God so loves our world that he gives us his only Son.

4

Vatican II: For the Life of the World

Revd Dr James Hanvey SJ

I Introduction: Situating the council

(Moral Theology) Nourished more on the teaching of the Bible, should shed light on the loftiness of the calling of the faithful in Christ and the obligation that is theirs of bearing fruit in charity for the life of the world.[1]

Most Catholics now live in a Church which is the fruit of the Council. Whatever position we adopt regarding the subsequent interpretation of the Second Vatican Council and the implementation of its acts, there is general agreement that it was and remains a unique event.[2] A significant element in this uniqueness lies in its rationale as well as the form of its decrees and Constitutions.[3]

---

[1]*The Decree on Priestly Formation*, Optatam Totus (1965), 16.
[2]For a concise discussion of the differing views, including the attempts to regularize the Council, see Massimo Faggioli, *Vatican II: The Battle for Meaning* (New York: Paulist Press, 2012). Especially Chapter 5, p. 91.
[3]Here, John O'Malley is surely correct when he argues for the new genre of the Council and its texts. See 'Vatican II: Did Anything Happen?', in *Theological Studies* 67 (2006), pp. 3–33. Also *Tradition and Transition: Historical Perspectives on Vatican Two* (Wilmington, DE: Michael Glazier, 1989). Also, David G. Schultenover (ed.), *Vatican Two: Did anything Happen?* (New York: Continuum, 2007), which contains O'Malley's original article and a number of responses. Still useful commentaries are: H. Vorgrimler (ed.), *Commentary on the Documents of Vatican II* (London/Freibourg: Burns and Oates/ Herder Herder, 1966), Volumes I (On *Lumen Gentium*) and V (On *Gaudium et Spes*).

Historically, Councils are usually called to correct error and reform the life of the Church. They normally formulate their acts in terms of anathemas and canons. As well as identifying, condemning and correcting a perceived error of life or doctrine in the Church they also help us locate a Council. This allows the reader to place the event historically and provide a framework for interpretation. The fact that Vatican II issued no anathemas and did not see itself as summoned to correct any errors, is both a problem and the key to understanding the Council and the challenge it continues to pose.

In eschewing the traditional conciliar form, Vatican II understood itself as 'pastoral'; moreover, it did not establish any central body to oversee its implementation and shape interpretations of is constitutions and decrees.[4] On the positive side this allows for two things: first, practically, the interpretation and implementation of the Council devolves much more to local hierarchies and schools of theology.

This reflects the genuinely international or ecumenical nature of the Council's participating bishops, and emerges in its growing awareness of national and local circumstances and cultures.[5] Granted that there is always the necessary oversight of the Office of Peter, local churches have much more flexibility to respond to the situations and cultures to which they minister.

Second: inevitably it generates a plurality of understandings and practices, all claiming some sort of legitimacy in the documents of the Council. With some urgency, the question then arises if the very nature of Catholic unity is not compromised and the authority of the Office of Peter as well as local hierarchies weakened? What appears as an experience of creativity and freedom immediately after the Council can quickly become an experience of chaos resulting in a real loss of clarity in structure and mission.[6] When we

---

[4]See Karl Rahner 'On the Theological Problems Entailed in a "Pastoral Constitution"', in *Theological Investigations* (New York: Herder and Herder, 1973), vol. X. Particularly insightful on the hermeneutical issues of the Council is Walter Kasper's essay, 'The Continuing Challenge of the 2nd Vatican Council', in *Theology of the Church*, trans. Margaret Kohl (New York: Crossroads, 1992), pp. 166–76.

[5]This finds expression within the Council documents in a number of places but especially *Lumen Gentium* 13 (LG) and *Ad Gentium* 22 (AD).

[6]Congar also notes that Councils have traditionally been prepared by a series of local councils and reform movements which help prepare and ease the subsequent reception. See Yves Congar's 'Renewal of the Spirit and Reform of the Institution',

combine this with the very profound theological reconceptualizing that the Council explicitly maps – the theologies of liturgy, the laity, collegiality, religious liberty, the new status of other Christian confessions, other religions and a repositioning of the Church *vis-à-vis* secular culture (national and international) – it is not surprising that the intoxication of *aggiornamento* can give way to the hangover of the day after![7] Post-conciliar papacies have expended considerable energy in providing interpretative frameworks for the Council while developing aspects of its teaching and vision. Benedict XVI has identified two approaches in terms of the hermeneutics of rupture and the hermeneutics of continuity.[8] Although Benedict argues correctly against seeing the Council as a 'rupture' and in favour of continuity we still need to appreciate how the Council understood itself in terms of continuity. In this respect it is clear that the idea of continuity which informs the Council is one of dynamic development. The hermeneutic of 'continuity' cannot and should not be used to normalize the Council and minimize its achievements, its vision or the tasks which its sets for the Church and the creative challenges which it still continues to propose. No reading of the Council can ignore that it commits us to the journey of history, to the task of 'renewing our mind' that we may more clearly see and live the incomprehensible and inexhaustible mystery of Christ and the grace of the triune life we are called to participate in even in our present historical existence (LG 48). This opens up the reality of the Church as the 'universal sacrament of salvation'. The Council initiates a process – theological, spiritual and practical – of which it is also a part. The Church is part of this history and that means it must not only understand its own need to change in order to be faithful to Christ and the mission entrusted to it, but also that it

---

in Alois Muller and Norbert Greinbacher (eds), *Concilium: Ongoing Reform of the Church* (New York: Herder and Herder, 1972), pp. 45–6. Having said that, we should note that the theology which informs the Council was well prepared in the thought of Congar, de Lubac, Rahner, Chenu and the theologians around them in what was called the *'nouvelle théologie'*.

[7]C. Theobald, 'Vatican II Confronts the Unknown Collegial Discernment of "the Signs of the Times"', in Silvia Scantena, Jon Sobrino and Dennis Gira (eds), *Concilium* (London: SCM Press, 2012/13), pp. 56–63.

[8]Address of His Holiness Pope Benedict XVI to the Roman Curia, 22 December 2005, http://www.vatican.va/holy_father/benedict_xvi/speeches/2005/december/documents/hf_ben_xvi_spe_20051222_roman-curia_en.html [accessed 12 March 2013].

can realize its own historical agency as the 'universal sacrament of salvation'.

If one of the most important achievements of the Council was its grasp and assimilation of the historical consciousness of modernity, it did this by rediscovering the dynamic nature of tradition and reading it within the scriptural horizon of salvation history. So, the dynamic of the Council still continues as we struggle not only to assimilate it, but to develop, deepen and apply its resources to ever new situations.

The second moment of reception

In this chapter I wish to suggest that we are now at a new point in the Council's reception and assimilation.[9] Indeed, it may well be that we are engaged in the second stage of the Council's reception if we count the Extraordinary Synod of 1985 as marking the end of the first stage.[10] If the first stage was marked by an explosion of revision, renewal and change and the inevitable struggles and tensions this produced, then the anniversaries marking the Council's opening and conclusion also allow for a new moment of reception. I do not suggest this simply because they are convenient dates but because the controversies about interpretation which the Extraordinary Synod hoped to quieten have grown.[11] Thanks to the excellent scholarship of a number of projects designed to gather not only the primary and secondary documents of the Council, but also many personal diaries and recollections, we now have a very complete record of the whole event. These factors, combined with the post-conciliar papal Magisterium and the work of many national conferences, have all expanded, interpreted and developed the Council's teachings. Of course, the world itself has not stood still. The changing geo-political reconfigurations, the impact of

---

[9]See also Hermann J. Pottmeyer, 'A New Phase in the Reception of Vatican Two: Twenty Years of Interpretation of the Council', in Giuseppe Alberigo, Jean-Pierre Jossua and Joseph A. Komonchak (eds), *The Reception of Vatican Two* (Washington, DC: Catholic University of America Press, 1987), pp. 27–43.

[10]Final Report of the Extraordinary Synod, 7 December 1985, *Enchiridion Vaticanum*. Also significant is the submission of the Bishops Conference of England and Wales in *The Tablet*, 3 August 1985 and the subsequent comment 'The Sound of Brakes' in 7 December 1985.

[11]See Faggioli, *Vatican II: The Battle for Meaning.*

globalization and information technology, combined with the substantial changes in cultural thought over fifty years, have an impact on the way we read and understand the Council.[12]

There is a second reason why in this particular moment of reception it is important to return to the texts. Here the task is not only to appreciate the limitations of the texts – limitations of which their authors were very much aware – but also their considerable achievements. In this sense, too, we can see that the Council must be read as the beginning of a new phase in the Church's self-understanding and development for which the theology is still being worked out.[13]

If the Extraordinary Synod 1985 celebrated and endorsed the Council (against Lefevrist claims that it was illegitimate), it also represented a narrowing of focus. While calling for a reading of the texts 'as a whole' and especially in the light of the four main constitutions, it also seemed to mark a turning inward in an attempt to determine both an authoritative interpretation of the Council and to address the tensions in the Church's life which have arisen in its wake. It is interesting to notice what the Synod stressed and what it overlooked or downplayed. The most significant example of this is the emphasis on the Church as mysterium and communion – undoubtedly central themes – as opposed to the important theme of 'the People of God' which runs through Lumen Gentium and other conciliar documents. The Church as the People of God was developed in a number of ways in post-conciliar theology.[14] However, there was a fear that it was interpreted in such a way as to 'democratize the Church'.[15] Moreover, the Synod seemed less inclined to reaffirm the Council's direct evangelical engagement with the secular world and its recognition of the signs of the Kingdom which that world also contains. In fact, it thought it necessary to place more emphasis on the cross in the pilgrim journey of the Church in the world, thus

---

[12]A significant example of this is the development of feminist thought and its significance for the society and the Church.

[13]See Yves Congar, *My Journal of the Council*, trans. Denis Minns et al. (Collegeville, MN: Liturgical Press, 2012), p. 556.

[14]This point is made several times by Jean-Marie Tillard in 'Final Report of the Last Synod, in Synod 1985 – An Evaluation', in Guiseppe Alberigo and James Provost (eds), *Concilium* (Edinburgh: T&T Clark, 1986), pp. 64–77.

[15]See J. Ratzinger, *Church, Ecumenism, Politics. New Endevors in Ecclesiology*, trans. Michael J. Miller et al. (San Francisco: Ignatius Press, 2008). Especially, chapter I, Appendix, p. 29ff.

reflecting the cultural and political shifts since the conclusion of the Council in 1965.[16]

To understand the full extent of this reading of the Church's nature and mission and the way in which it also reorients it to the world would require a more detailed exposition of the major texts than is possible within the limits of this essay. Although each represents a work in progress, I believe that we can begin to see the principle outlines if we read *Lumen Gentium* and *Gaudium et Spes* together. In doing this I believe that we see unifying theological structures which themselves establish an internal hermeneutic which is important to grasp if we wish to interpret the Council in a complete way. It also enables us to identify more accurately the achievement they represent and the work which they continue to ask us to do.[17]

II The mystery of the church – Being in mission

Before Vatican II, the Church was predominantly thought of as a *perfecta societatis*.[18] This definition was developed by Robert Bellarmine partly in response to the criticisms of the Protestant Reformers and partly in terms of the politico-theological status of the Church at the time. This largely juridical model of the Church was tempered by the ecclesiology of the 'Mystical Body' promoted by Pius XII in the encyclical *Mystici Corporis Christi* published in 1943. Even so, both ways of understanding the Church – always understood as the Roman Catholic Church – still emphasized its hierarchical constitution, governed by the Pope, and sanctified through the proper administration of the sacraments. The first chapter of Lumen Gentium not only begins by proclaiming Christ and setting the gift of redemption which he offers within a universal horizon, it introduces a new way of speaking and therefore thinking about the Church.

---

[16]For a sophisticated hermeneutic of the Council, see Christoph Theobald, SJ, *La réception de concile Vatican II, Accéder à la source* (Paris: Cerf, 2009).

[17]GS 40/42 explicitly presupposes LG.

[18]For Bellarmine's influential definition, see De Defin. Ecc. Book 3, Chapter 2. But Bellarmine also argues that the Church is animated by the interior gifts of the Holy Spirit: faith, hope, love.

The dominant ecclesiologies of the *societas perfecta* and the Mystical Body are situated within the Trinitarian economy of salvation.[19] In this way the dynamic theological architecture of Christological and Pneumatological can play a more creative and critical part in shaping ecclesiology. By highlighting the Trinitarian economy the Church is placed within the unfolding of salvation history. This allows the Christian community to appreciate its own historicity and it also makes explicit the unity of its identity and mission grounded in the missions of the Son and the Holy Spirit. Not only is the life and the historical consciousness of the Church shaped in this way but so too are its structures, especially those which are from the *jus divinum* or divine origin. If the Church's historical reality is now seen within the eschatological horizon of the Divine economy, its mission is a participation in and agent of that economy, determined to the 'telos' of God's salvific will.[20] There is a supernatural unity between the destiny of every human being ordered to participation in the divine life and the essence/mission of the Church.[21] The logic of the incarnational dynamic at work here places the Church ever more deeply in the world as part of its own redeemed destiny – not only as the universal sacrament of salvation but, in some sense, the sacrament of humanity – the Kingdom still present in mystery.[22] Without compromising the analogical principle of the fourth Lateran Council, the eschatological horizon of history is known and anticipated in the truth of faith which the Spirit confers so that it is perceived and lived (in an incomplete but real way) within history: eschatology shapes ontology and historical existence.[23] Within the texts it is interesting to observe the way the frequent kerygmatic or creedal narratives function.

---

[19]LG 7; also *Gaudium et Spes* 24/32 (GS).

[20]This theme is carried through in other documents of the Council, especially *Ad Gentes*.

[21]See Hans Urs von Balthasar, 'Konzil Des Heiligen Geistes', in *Spiritus Creator, Skizzen zur Theologie* (Einsiedeln: Johannes Verlag, 1967), pp. 218–36. See especially, p. 219ff.

[22]LG 3. The effect of this is also to relativize the Church's institutional form and make it subject to the mystery of Christ and His Kingdom. Again, this places the Church epistemologically as well as structurally within an evolutionary trajectory.

[23]'The resemblance between the Creator and the creature is such that their still greater dissimilarity cannot fail to be observed' *Decretalis* III also St Thomas, *Quaest, disp. De Scientia Dei*, a. 11. If this principle is not recognized, then there is a danger of a Hegelian fusion of the Trinity and history.

They are not just repetitions but act as structural recollections of salvation history. As confessions of the Church's faith situated it, they are epistemic epiphanies which disclose the movement of salvation history within human history. They demonstrate that the memoria Christi, especially in its liturgical form, orients the community in a transcendence towards the future which only God can realize. As with the exodus of Israel from the captivity of Egypt to the theophany of Sinai, so the People of God, the New Israel, live out of the supreme exodus of Christ's resurrection from the dead: a reality within history which also shapes it through the new law of the Spirit.[24] This is reflected in the way in which the mission of the Church is actually a performance of its identity-essence in history – it has no option but to be in the world and to be at the heart of humanity as it lives out of the incarnate mystery of Christ.

The soteriological nature of communio/solidarity

It is clear that for Lumen Gentium, the Church cannot be understood apart from the mystery of Christ. Just as in Christ there is no separation between person and mission, so too in the Church there is no division between identity and mission. If, as we have seen, Christ is also the 'telos' of humanity and the fulfilment of what it means to be human, so too humanity must have an ecclesial destiny. It is in this context that the core theme of solidarity/communio begins to surface.[25] Human nature is not social by accident or purely by utilitarian necessity. It is social by its very nature, and only in living out his or her relational constitution can the individual flourish. There is now perceived a convergence of the human vocation to life with God – individually and in solidarity with all humanity – and the Church, 'All men are called to this union with Christ, who is the light of the world, from whom we go forth, through whom we live, and toward whom our whole life strains.'[26] The mystery of solidarity as an anthropological-social reality must also be grasped as a soteriological reality if it is to be fully understood. In this way,

---

[24]This is especially evident in LG Chapter 8, and 4; 8; 13; 42. Also see GS 45.
[25]See especially GS 32.
[26]LG 3; GS 11.

the Church finds itself ontologically impressed in the very nature of humanity ordered and summoned to union with the triune God.[27] The true depth of communio/solidarity receives its most profound and beautiful exposition in Chapter VIII of Lumen Gentium which expounds our 'communio' with Church in glory.

There is here a cosmic dimension to the Church's reality and mission as well. 'Solidarity' encompasses the whole of creation; the healing of the wound of sin becomes a restoration of not only of the unity of all women and men, but the restoration and regeneration of humanity's relation to creation; our vocation of loving, respectful stewardship of creation's grace. Both of these dimensions further stand under the eschatological nature of the Church's life. The Church lives towards the future and the consummation of Christ's glory in history. As such it lives always beyond itself as pilgrim (viator) and possessor of the fullness of Christ and his truth (comprehensor). In this sense, too, in its very mission the Church possesses its being in becoming. When we grasp this, we see that that mission is not just something that the Church does, but something that the Church is – mission discloses the unity of performance (witness and life) and essence. Yet, precisely because this is lived in an eschatological transcendence towards the triune future, it cannot collapse its being and essence so as to abolish its historical existence which is the field of its missionary/pastoral life.[28] In other words, the Church must always live in faith from the gift of the Holy Spirit in obedience to God's will which it cannot foreclose. Not only does this constitute the way in which the Church is marked epistemologically and existentially in history by the kenosis of the Cross, its eschatological character means that it cannot secure its own being. Far from being a limitation in history, it becomes the source of the Church's generative freedom.[29]

What becomes clear is that the mission of the Church is not something independent from its being which is grounded in the Trinitarian economy. Lumen Gentium will express this in a variety of different ways through developing traditional metaphors of the

---

[27]Explicitly developed in GS 22. See also GS 24 and LG 48.

[28]LG 5 and Rahner, *Theological Investigations*.

[29]*Dei Verbum* (The Constitution on Divine Revelation) 2, 5, 7, 8, 9 and especially 21, 23. Here, *Dei Verbum* is also integral to understanding both *Lumen Gentium* and *Gaudium et Spes*.

Church as well as the notion that in some way the Church continues the soteriological dynamic of the incarnation and resurrection.[30]

Guided by this Christological focus and inherent unity of being and mission, the ecclesiology of Lumen Gentium moves us away from any temptation to triumphalism or to a defensive withdrawal from the world. The underlying image is that of 'servant' which is further developed in Gaudium et Spes where it determines the fundamental mode of the Church's mission for the world.[31] The motif of humble, loving service to humanity marks an extraordinary recovery of the Church's way of being in the world, even when it experiences that world as hostile. Yet, it does not imply any renunciation of the Church's epistemological privilege in knowing Christ and God's salvific will for his creation. Rather, it is this very knowledge which is the source of the community's prophetic mission: caritas Christi urget nos. (Cor. 5.14) Again it is a sort of performance of the Christological foundation of the community's life: the Church renders service as a sort of imitatio Christi (LG 3).[32] Imitato also informs the Church's understanding of her suffering in and with the world. Ultimately it situates the Christian community in the salvific mystery of the cross.[33] Within the dogmatic constitution (Lumen Gentium) we are orientated to the pastoral one (Gaudium et Spes), without which the full ecclesiological achievement of the Council would be deficient.[34]

The laity and the sanctification of the secular

This sketch of the overarching theological structure in Lumen Gentium and its significance for Gaudium et Spes can be easily submerged in the other themes of the documents even though

---

[30]See LG 8 and 52. Also Mühlen, 'Das Verhältnis zwischen Reinkarnation und Kirche in den Aussagen des Vaticanum II', in *Theologie und Glaube*, 55 (1965), pp. 171–90.

[31]GS 3; 11.

[32]The idea of service is also the dominant theme in the treatment of the hierarchical Church, in LG Chapter III.

[33]See especially LG 3, 8 and GS 41, 42.

[34]Here, the distinction between 'dogmatic' and 'pastoral' becomes important not only for the juridical and theological reading of the two Constitutions but how we understand their relationship. Rahner, *Theological Investigations*.

it is crucial to their own development. Increasingly, it becomes clear that the Council's sense of the activity of the Holy Spirit in the Church, in humanity and in the world, is an underlying presupposition of its thinking. Unfortunately, neither in Lumen Gentium nor in Gaudium et Spes is it given the systematic treatment which is needed. I shall return to this in my concluding observations, however at this point, it will be sufficient to identify its significance in the treatment of the laity in Lumen Gentium which is foundational for Gaudium et Spes. There are two subtle but related aspects of this: the mission/vocation of the laity in the sanctification of the secular and the work of the Spirit in the world beyond the visible Church. The former can be seen not only in the specific attention given to the theology of the laity in Lumen Gentium, chapter IV but especially in chapter V: The Universal Call to Holiness. Not only does this mark a significant development over the pre-conciliar understanding of the laity and their proper mission, it opens the way for a reconceptualization of the secular which is carried through to Gaudium et Spes.[35] In addition to mapping out a new theology of the laity, it opens the way to exploring the ontology of holiness and sanctification as an active transformational reality within the world as the repair and generation of the good.

Through the theology of the laity developed into the universal call to holiness we are moved beyond a tendency to think of holiness as a quality inhering only in the individual. If the Church is herself 'holy' this holiness is not simply the aggregate of individual holiness: the Church is a communio of holiness. Moreover, the life of every Christian is not only a salvific sign before the world of Christ's promise in fulfilment, but is already a communio/solidarity with the whole of humanity:

> All this holds true not only for Christians, but for all men of good will in whose hearts grace works in an unseen way. For, since Christ died for all men, and since the ultimate vocation of man is in fact one, and divine, we ought to believe that the Holy Spirit in a manner known only to God offers to every man the possibility of being associated with this paschal mystery.[36]

---

[35]GS 12ff.
[36]GS 22, 92.

The Christian, as a person and also in the community of the Church, is not only a sign of hope of the redeemed destiny of all humanity. As individual and as community, the Christian marks the ontological difference between a lost and despairing world and one that, through all its tribulations, can trust in God's promise. It is also a testimony to the Council's vision of the dynamism of God's salvific will in Christ and the action of the Holy Spirit that there are no barriers to the offer of God's love other than those which are erected through wilful refusal. The deeper evolutionary dynamic is, here, understood to express a theological dynamic of salvation. The Council traces the movement of salvation history within the secular history of humanity and its fractured progress disturbed by sin where the vocation and the grace of the laity become integral to the Church's mission and are an active expression of it. Here we move beyond the sacramental actions of the Church into the sanctifying action of the lives of the faithful.[37] Both through the actions of 'ordinary' Christian life and through the work of the Holy Spirit, the secular, far from being a space of God's enforced absence, becomes the realm of God's presence:

> They live in the ordinary circumstances of family and social life, from which the very web of their existence is woven. They are called there by God that by exercising their proper function and led by the spirit of the Gospel they may work for the sanctification of the world from within as a leaven. In this way they may make Christ known to others, especially by the testimony of a life resplendent in faith, hope and charity. Therefore, since they are tightly bound up in all types of temporal affairs it is their special task to order and to throw light upon these affairs in such a way that they may come into being and then continually increase according to Christ to the praise of the Creator and the Redeemer.[38]

By implication, too, the faithful now have a theological signifi-cance and their lives are a theological resource for the Church and

---

[37]Sin frustrates human endeavour in every field and prevents the deeper solidarity of persons (GS 25).
[38]LG 31, 33, 36.

its discernment of the truth by which it lives. Of course, the very witness of the Christian lives lived with integrity in the unspectacular 'ordinary' exposes the de-sacralized 'world' deliberately constructed and lived against God's presence and design (GS 37). Thus Christian presence and action highlights the 'drama' of human existence and the fundamental nature of the choice that is placed before humanity. The 'epistemological privilege' of Christ gives the Church and its members a unique understanding of the consequences of sin for humanity and thus intensifies the Church's soteriological mission and the mission of every individual member (GS 37).

These themes are taken up and explored in Gaudium et Spes in its treatment of atheism and sin. Yet what emerges is not a Church that either prescinds from the drama or is immune to it. Rather we are presented with a Church already a servant of the mystery of the Kingdom and engaged in the performance of the grace of Christ in history. It is a Church which has committed itself in every way to the salvation of humanity and so it understands its work as one of bringing to fruition the good that is sought and achieved (LG 13).

A Christological humanism

Even from this brief treatment it will be clear that the anthropology implicit in Lumen Gentium becomes the centre of Gaudium et Spes. It represents a major hermeneutical tool for the dialogue it seeks with the world. Taking its Christocentric vision at its point of engagement, the Council holds that humanity can neither understand itself or have any hope of realizing its potential if it reads itself independently from God. If the secular constructs itself without recognizing this, under the assumption that human emancipation is completed in absolute independence from God, then it cannot ultimately achieve the goods it desires or the human flourishing that it seeks. We have seen how in Lumen Gentium this humanism is also a profoundly ecclesial one that is already a soteriological expression of the grace of Christ and the Holy Spirit active in every human life expressed in historical agency. Blending a number of traditions, not only Augustinian, Thomistic, personalist and existentialist, Gaudium et spes produces theological anthropology which can respond to the secular world.[39] The Christian humanism which it outlines represents a close engagement with the anthropologies of the secular Enlightenment and the atheisms of modernity. It offers the possibility of rethinking itself in such a way that it can overcome its own aporias.

In both constitutions it becomes clear that there is a determination to move from static, essentialist, ahistorical categories of thought into those that are scriptural, dynamic and open to both the contingency of history and its telos revealed in Christ. This produces a 'dynamic, open ontology'. This also is the context of the Council's reading of the world, especially human society, which it sees as undergoing rapid change and transformation.[40] But the change identified is also understood in terms of an anthropology: it is the product of human agency and therefore it stands as, in some sense, a self-expressive creation of human desires, needs, conflicts and aspirations. Culture is a human creation which also reveals what humanity is.[41] If the essence of the human person is secured in the imago dei/imago Christi, it must be understood teleologically in terms of vocation and destiny. Lived out as these are within existence and history, not only are the individual and society determined by material and physical finiteness but by the progressive opportunities and closures occasioned in choices that are made. In a very real sense we are shaped by these choices; they express our finite freedom within history. However, as well as response, freedom is self-disclosure: our choices reveal our sense of who we are and the meaning we seek. As well as being manifest in individual choices, freedom expresses itself through the social structures and histories our choices (collective and well as individual) create (GS 31). Gaudium et Spes understands culture as such a creation. In this way every culture reveals its anthropological assumptions; it reveals whether it understands the *telos* of human existence or merely instrumentalizes the human to meet other purposes (GS 21).

---

[39]For a discussion of these schools as the Council and their significance for its subsequent reading and reception, see Faggioli, *Vatican Two and the Battle for Meaning*, p. 66ff. But there is also a strong existentialist/personalist dimension to the treatment, especially in placing the human person before the mystery of death which conditions the search for meaning. See also GS 18.

[40]GS 5, 6, 42, 54.

[41]GS 53ff.

If the Enlightenment recognizes that the person is an end and never a means, then it recognizes not only a principle but a truth that is profoundly Christian. The Council argues, however, that this most fundamental of truths and all that depends upon it can only be secured by Christ. If the secular not only seeks to exclude Christ and Christianity from its self-understanding, then it will also jeopardize the human as well. Only in the fullness of body, mind, will and spirit can we come to understand the *telos* or destiny to which we are called. The 'telos' or 'destiny' which marks every human life is not a mere hypothetical or abstract construct. It is an active dimension of our existence and experience. The Council chooses to explore this in terms of the 'vocation' with which all are endowed. As we explore this we also come to see that this 'telos' is experienced as a vocation both to self-realization and to participation in the Divine life (GS 10). Theology and anthropology have an existential unity as well as theoretical one because both are united in the person of Christ who is the 'alpha and omega' of humanity. It is only in and through Him that the enigma of our meaning and purpose, and hence of our freedom in history, can be perceived (GS 22). Our positive response to Him, therefore, can never be against our nature or our freedom but always the grace of participating in our own becoming.

As we have seen, against the sovereign self of the secular Enlightenment and modernity, the Council proposes the relational constitution of the human person. Here, we will recall the way in which Lumen Gentium prepares the way for this by showing how this relational constitution of the human person is ordered to communio/solidarity with all its moral, social and political implications. Our apparent incompleteness is not only the key to our social nature but it is rooted theologically as well. The command to love God and our neighbour is not just a moral rule but an ontological imperative. In so far as the priority of love is written into our nature we understand ourselves truly as imago dei. Love then is finally understood to be the goal of human freedom. [42]

However, positive though this theological anthropology is, the Council does not propose an idealized or utopian vision of the human person or human society. In its recognition of the instability of human nature and the human capacity for self-deception, the Council reflects an Augustinian realism. Its treatment of sin is

---

[42]See, for example, GS Chapter II and also LG 40.

integral to its anthropology. The *mysterium iniquitatis* cannot be reduced to categories of deficiency, social dysfunction or historical circumstances which translate into human behaviour and social habits. They may surely be symptoms but it is a mistake to treat them as cause. To do so still perpetuates the illusion that human nature has within itself all the resources it needs to liberate and perfect itself. The belief that humanity can be hero of its own soteriology is part of the *incurvatus in se* that marks the refusal of God and the refusal of the *communio* which only God can bring about. Not only does it jeopardize the individual but the whole of humanity and the goods of creation as well. Sin also corrupts our desires as well as corrupting our freedom, hence the self and society we are able to express and create. In other words, whether in the nobility of its vocation or the depravity of actions humanity needs grace; it needs the God who comes to us in Christ if it is to be itself. This is not an oppressive dependency designed to keep humanity in subjection that some forms of atheism have maintained. Rather, the Council argues, it is a restoration of an authentic freedom; it not only recognizes the wounded nature of our finitude but the gift of our relational transcendence. Freedom, if it is to genuinely serve us, must be ordered to love and to truth. This is the intuition that lies at the heart of every conscience and whether a person is explicitly Christian or not, in so far as they are true to their conscience they are true to their ultimate vocation to the God who is 'the Way, the Truth and the Life' – the Trinitarian God whose essence in Love. Freedom, too, needs to be redeemed and sanctified if it is to be a genuine freedom. It needs to come under the power of the Holy Spirit (GS 38). Once again we can see how the 'pastoral' nature of Gaudium et Spes is actually a systematic soteriological reading of world and the human activity which shapes it.[43]

The theological anthropology outlined in Lumen Gentium and in Gaudium et Spes is a discreet but creative response to the central themes of the Enlightenment and modernity. Often used to critique and reject Catholicism, these themes now find themselves integrated into a Christian vision. Arguably, it not only deepens

---

[43]For a nuanced discussion of these themes in the light of *Gaudium et Spes*, see Henri de Lubac 'The Total Meaning of Man and the World', in *Communio*, 35 (Winter), 2008. Translated from 'Athéisme et sens de l'homme: une double requête de Gaudium et Spes', in *Oeuvres Completes*, vol. 4 (Paris: Cerf, 2006), pp. 471–500.

them, but provides the resources from within the Catholic tradition to rescue the noble inspirations of the secular traditions from their aporias and the collapse into the incoherence of relativism or the despair of nihilism – the crisis of modernity. This is most evident in the way in which the Council develops the emancipatory project of secular modernity and re-reads it through its Christology and ecclesiology to produce a dynamic theology of the human person: 'Whoever follows after Christ, the perfect man, becomes himself more of a man'.[44]

It is in the light of its theological anthropology and its revisioning of the secular that we can now place part II of Gaudium et Spes. Whatever its deficiencies, seen within the theological perspectives we have been exploring, it looks less like a pragmatic agenda of obviously good causes and more like the tentative suggestions for the practical working out of the soteriological dynamic which is part of the Church's mission of service in the world. The Church is present in history not only as the sacrament of salvation but the servant of the mystery of the Kingdom. It is through historical structures, especially in all the fields of national and international systems that the conditions for the realization of human dignity which carries the imago dei/imago Christi – now seen to be not simply a state but also a task – must be worked out. If that dignity is to be honoured, it needs new economic, social and political systems of relationships governed by universally recognized legal and ethical structures, for example, human rights, which even partially begin to secure measures of justice and peace.

From the perspective of the Council's anthropological vision, religious freedom is not an appendix added because of the Church's vested interest in humanity's relationship to God. Religious freedom is integral to the human search not only for God but for humanity itself. If it is lost or diminished, then the conditions for the possibility of authentic human flourishing are frustrated and endangered. Humanity becomes imprisoned philosophically in systems predicated upon a false and falsifying understanding of the human person; it is trapped in social and economic systems which create the illusion of freedom and security but in fact have a purely instrumental approach to people.

---

[44] GS 41: 'Quicumque Christum sequitur, Hominem perfectum, et ipse magis homo fit'.

Likewise, the Council's emphasis on freedom ordered to truth and love, combined with its teaching on the sanctuary of conscience, is an ultimate line of resistance against all totalitarian claims upon the human and the colonization of the interior as well as exterior spaces of human existence. Hence the Council's desire, in line with the tradition of Catholic social teaching, for the correct ordering of the public/State, civic and private realms.[45] Moreover, the consistent attention to the rights and claims of the poor, the marginalized and oppressed and their need of economic and political justice is more than an agenda for social reconstruction, necessary though that is. It is part of the commitment that the Church has to the Gospel of the Kingdom, grounded in its Christology and anthropology, especially its understanding of the salvific solidarity/communio of humanity. It is not difficult to see here an underlying theological trajectory that runs from Lumen Gentium to Gaudium et Spes which helps us understand how the Church is actively the sacrament of salvation effective not only for its own members but for all humanity through the charity which takes flesh in the healing deeds of service for the life of the world.

III Conclusion: Possibilities, problems and aporias – living up to the task of Vatican II

In this chapter, I have attempted to outline the theology which connects both Lumen Gentium and Gaudium et Spes, stressing the unity of the nature of the Church and its mission. In a relatively short essay it is not possible to do justice to the complexity of the documents which deal with a variety of significant themes across a wide range of fields. It is clear, however, that there is a theological arc which connects them and it is important to appreciate this if we are to recognize the Council's achievement and carry forward the task which it sets.

Of course, in addition to providing us with rich theological resources, Gaudium et Spes and Lumen Gentium present us

---

[45]GS 73–6 and also in the Council decree, *Dignitatis Humanae*.

with many aspects which remain incomplete or problematic. For example, neither constitution had much to say about women beyond the cultural roles at the time, nor had the Council absorbed the penetrating feminist critiques of society which were emerging at the time and became politically as well as philosophically influential. In terms of the Church's own life, the post-conciliar years have not only demonstrated the international significance of the Papacy, but highlighted the need to develop effective forms of collegiality which remains underdeveloped. The theological and practical tension here lies with a papacy still largely determined by an ultramontanist theology and the political models of a nineteenth-century monarchy. If the Church is to achieve the genuine communion which John Paul II saw as essential to face the challenges of the twenty-first century, then this remains a critical task. With it goes the recovery of other sources of legitimate theological authorities within the life of the Church, for example, the teaching authorities of Catholic theologians, the witness of religious life and the expertise and theological 'sensum' of the laity. As yet, the largely unrecognized theological resource of a secular world and the particular wisdom that it has to offer the Church remains untapped in any formal way. I have suggested that all of these possibilities are hinted at in the Council. However, in these closing observations, I wish to briefly identity three areas which offer themselves as significant sites for further theological development.

Reclaiming the secular

I have attempted to argue that a significant achievement of the Council was its reclamation of the secular. Yet, to some, the reclamation was more like a capitulation. They saw all the errors of modernity condemned by the Magisterium before the Council now accepted as authentic teaching. To be sure, the texts do not present us with a completed thesis and therefore there are lacunae and pitfalls for the rash. But to see the Council as the triumph of secularism represents a failure to grasp the depth of the Council's theological engagement with it. Vatican II offers the secular another way of thinking of itself. Faithful to the logic of the incarnation which actually creates the world which it presupposes, Lumen Gentium and Gaudium et Spes place the Christian community in a new relation to the secular without compromising its prophetic difference. Yet, none of this leads to a Christian utopia because the Council always understands history within the drama of the cross lived within the eschatological horizon of God's future. By way of explanation, the intuition of the Council is to take up the emancipatory project of modernity, with its secular soteriology, offer a critique of why it cannot succeed and then propose its own soteriological vision. In this, it is able to indicate how all the principle themes of modernity's emancipatory project – its search for the lasting human good – can not only be preserved but deepened and secured when seen as seeds of the Kingdom and read in terms of dynamic of salvation history. In this way, the Council not only succeeds in avoiding the modernist error identified by Pascendi, it also refuses the liberal Protestant assimilation of the Gospel to the norms and fashions of a particular age and social status quo.[46]

As we have seen, Gaudium et Spes places a Christological anthropology at the centre of this bold conceptual and practical move. In a significant way, the consequence is to shift the Church's own public engagement with culture: in so far as it witnesses to Christ, it carries the 'memory' and the truth of what it is to be human. It could not be otherwise, given the Church's faith in the person of Christ, divine and human. Though not abandoning the language of natural law – the traditional language of public reason – it opens up a new site of public discourse in terms of the nature, meaning and purpose of the human person and human life. In doing so, it creates a powerful but problematic cultural, philosophical and political front.[47] Part of the problem lies in the fact that the question about the human person is often obscured in the pragmatic and ideological battles of policy and politics. The Church needs to develop fresh ways of engaging public discourse which do not trap it in these disputes if its salvific dialogue with culture is to bear fruit. Often the public stance of the Church can be misconstrued as self-interested or self-defensive of its teachings and practices.

On the one hand, there is the danger that the Church comes to be regarded as just another lobby which weakens its concern for the

---

[46]See Pope Pius X's encyclical *Pascendi Dominici Gregis* (1907).
[47]In this respect, the writings and witness of John Paul II develop in theory and in practice the new possibilities that the Council opens up.

common good. On the other, the Christian community can become so caught up in the immediacy of political tactics and strategies and the particular cultural sites of dispute raised to inflated symbolic status, that it forgets the greater horizon of its vision and the always urgent need of justice – at all levels – for the poor, weak, vulnerable and marginal.

Not only does theological and social anthropology of the Council renew the Church with a powerful vision of the human person, it also gives it the means to question society about the meaning and purpose of politics itself and the various systems – economic, social, educational etc. – that develop from it. If there is a Christian vision of the secular as the realm of human flourishing, then there is also a Christian vision of the plural ways in which this can be sought and expressed. Here, the question of religious freedom as constitutive of a complete anthropology rather than a pragmatic political or social arrangement needs to be established. This presents a direct question to the secular state: how does it preserve a genuine public space which allows for the many different voices in search of the common human good? The problem is not about plural notions as to what constitutes that good, but the way in which a secular ideology can become the basis of the state's judgements and policies while believing that it is neutral because it is not religious.[48] Both for the Church and for the secular state the Council offers an alternative to the conflicts and aporias that occur due to false or distorting frameworks that define their relationships. The Christian community needs to think through the theology of the secular which is outlined in the Council and in doing so, trust that it will come to a deeper appropriation of the Trinitarian mystery from which it lives.

Kenosis of the church and communio

The most radical theology in Gaudium et Spes and Lumen Gentium is that of kenosis. This is especially so when it is understood to be the normal mode of the Church's existence in its own internal life and in its life in the world. The theology of kenosis is largely

---

[48]See J. McClure and C. Taylor, *Secularism and Freedom of Conscience* (Harvard: Harvard University Press, 2011).

implicit and hence it has not received the attention it deserves in terms of ecclesiology. The groundwork for an ecclesiology of kenosis has already been laid in Lumen Gentium. We have seen how it interprets the Church through the Christological paradigm of the incarnation and the person of Christ. Kenosis unfolds as the essence of the Trinitarian economy and so the Church, which is itself the fruit of this economy, is marked by it in every aspect of its life and mission. In so far as the divine kenosis is the highest manifestation of God's own nature as triune love, so the kenosis of the Church is also a performative witness in the world and to the world of God's salvific and regenerative self-communication. This has profound implications.

Running implicitly throughout the Council's texts, kenosis is used to critique and transform our understanding of power and the way in which it is exercised. Kenosis is integral to the soteriology of the Kingdom because it is metanoia of power to the service of love concretized in the other, even when they are our enemy. In this way kenosis redeems power by refusing to allow it to become the assertion of the self – personal, social or institutional – over the other. From the subjection of the other it requires us to see and preserve the other as subject. Not only is kenosis liberative of the other but also of the self because it restores to the self the freedom of transcendence which is productive of the good in love. Both in the actions and in the teachings of Jesus we see this over and over again. All genuine acts of kenosis through its reversal of power presents a 'krisis' – destabilizing and exposing judgement – for systems constructed on power determined by self-interest and subjection of others and the goods of creation. Not only is kenosis the inner core of communio/solidarity but the antidote to the incurvatus in se which characterizes the destructive instrumentalizations and alienation of sin.

If the divine condescension in Christ manifests the supreme freedom of God in love to be for us, so our *imitatio Christi* becomes a salvific epiphany of the Kingdom in personal and social space. Ontologically, epistemologically and ethically it prioritizes the good of the other over self and self-interest. In doing so, kenosis opens up a new realm of possibilities – reconciliation, forgiveness, justice, peace, gift and self-sacrificing love. The mystery of grace at the heart of the divine kenosis in which the Church is constituted and eucharistically marked, is that it is generative of the new life of the

Kingdom. It restores and reorders relationships, hence is generative of communio, and it also opens up the new possibilities and spaces for humanity. It has its own ascesis, its ordering to the new law of love and is guided by the ever-unfolding truth of Christ.

It is one thing, however, to articulate a theology of kenosis and another to live it. The radically subversive yet liberating power that the grace of kenosis brings needs to be worked out and experienced in the praxis of history; in the engagement with the realities of personal, social, political, economic and material life. It is always at risk of wanting to claim or preserve its power in worldly terms, often believing that this is the best way it can influence and work for the common good. Yet, this may also be the way in which it sacrifices what is the unique gift of grace that it alone brings to the world – a love that expresses itself in self-gift and is free from all self-interest because it lives a 'consecrated love', a love which is the life of the Holy Spirit. The Church that lives out of kenosis will be a Church that lives out of its poverty – a poverty which it experiences in every aspect of its life. Constantly it will have to renew the discovery that it is this very gift of poverty that makes it a Church very free and unafraid in history.

In terms of its own internal life, this kenosis also marks a radical change in the understanding power, how it is exercised and the nature of status. It will certainly be integral to any theology of the laity and a holiness which is active and transformative within the structures of the secular. However, it must also have the same transformative effect on the Church's own structures, especially those which are 'jus divinum' and, therefore, grounded in God's own design for his community. Lumen Gentium consistently speaks of the hierarchical Church in terms of service. If this is to be more than a moral and spiritual exhortation, then it needs to be lived out and experienced in the practice of ecclesial life. Kenosis requires us to be creative in finding ways which shape the praxis and organizational structure of the operational life of the community. Kenosis becomes the habitus of the Church in so far as that it becomes incarnated in the institutional life of the People of God. The communio which is the effect of kenosis provides both the theological and practical context for deepening the reality of collegiality, making it both effective and affective. At all these levels the Council points us towards the deep work of 'renovatio' that still needs to be done.

The Holy Spirit

It would be impossible to read the Council documents, especially *Lumen Gentium* and *Gaudium et Spes*, and not be struck by the theology of the Holy Spirit that informs them. The Holy Spirit is the key to the ecclesial life they propose. In many ways, however, it remains a theology which still needs to be addressed. If in Vatican II the Church experiences 'a new Pentecost' as many have suggested, then Ormond Rush is surely correct when he says that the Council 'now requires of us a new pneumatology, that is, a new theology of how the Holy Spirit works'.[49] Without a more developed and integrated theology of the Spirit at work ad intra and ad extra we will never be able to realize the possibilities the Council opens up. This is especially urgent for the revisioning of the secular which we have identified as one of the major achievements of the Council but it also applies to the way in which we come to understand contemporary forms of practical (and theoretical) atheisms.[50]

I have suggested that these three sites highlighted by the texts of Lumen Gentium and Gaudium et Spes offer new and urgent fields of development for the life and mission of the Church. Claims have been made for the importance of other themes which may be more immediate. Whatever areas we come to regard as central, it must surely be obvious that our understanding of the Council and its reception is not concluded; it is a work still in progress. If we are to do justice to the nobility of this work, then the burden of this paper is simply a plea that we return 'ad fontes' to the great texts of the Council and the journey in faith, hope, love and prayer they call us to – *Veni Creator Spiritus!*

---

[49]O. Rush, *Still Interpreting Vatican II* (Mahwah, NJ: Paulist Press, 2004), p. 26. See also Léon-Joseph Suenens, *A New Pentecost?*, trans. Francis Martin (New York: Seabury, 1975) and Thomas Hughson, SJ, 'Interpreting Vatican II: A New Pentecost', in *Theological Studies*, 69 (2008), pp. 3–37.

[50]For the freedom of the Church and its presence in the secular, see M. Kehl, 'Kirche – Sakrament des Geistes, in Gegenwart des Geistes: Aspekt der Pneumatologie', in Walter Kasper et al. (eds), *Questiones Disputate*, vol. 85 (Fribourg: Herder and Herder, 1979), pp. 155–80.

5

A Vision for a Living Liturgy: Past, Present, and Future – Sacrosanctum Concilium

Mgr Timothy Menezes

Introduction to Vatican II

I will begin with two reflections that might help to put the fiftieth anniversary of the Second Vatican Council into a realistic context. First is the story that is often told by one of my parish priests, with whom I worked soon after my priestly ordination. He had been a student for the priesthood, in Rome, during the Council. He still speaks of the students trying to make sense of what the Council was all about, what was happening. Some of the students were on hand to transport bishops to and from the Vatican – about a 15-minute drive away from the English College. And, more than anything, they were very much aware that something big was happening. On one occasion, he recalls, an English bishop spoke to the whole student body about his experiences so far at the Council sessions. It was, in fact, Archbishop Francis Grimshaw, the Archbishop of Birmingham, who was representing the English Bishops on the liturgical commission working at the Council sessions. He acknowledged a degree of uncertainty about how it was unfolding and where it was going, but one thing he delivered with absolute conviction: 'I can assure you of one thing…that never during your lives will you hear the Canon of the Mass in English'. A matter of months later, the canon, and indeed the rest of the Mass was heard in English, and it has been heard in English by many ever since.

I will offer a second reflection. In September 1988 I began my studies for the priesthood at Oscott College in Birmingham. A priest I knew in my home parish asked me what the students were reading these days, what the latest theology books were. I was new to all of this. I had looked at a few students' bookshelves with some envy that they were so full, and I still had little to show for my early days. I told him one or two things I had seen and remember saying to him, 'some have got the Vatican II documents'. Remember, when filling shelf space was your primary aim, they certainly filled some space. The priest replied '*some* of them? I very much hope that *all* of them have got the Vatican II documents!' Having myself taught liturgy at Oscott College, our diocesan seminary, for the past 13 years, it is true that *Sacrosanctum Concilium* (henceforth, 'SC') articles 1–20 were the first expectation for student reading and are still a foundation for the study of the Church's liturgy today.

Perhaps these reflections are an illustration of two aspects of a contemporary view of the Council. First, my relationship with Vatican II which began 25 years after it. I never knew a pre-conciliar Church. So, there will be something very different from those above the age of say, 60, whose comparisons of before, during and since will underpin today's view. Second, my parish priest's recollections from Rome in the 1960s.

Also, I would like to give a word of caution about terms such as 'the Spirit of Vatican II' or 'the Mind of the Church'; less still speaking of the Council as 'the worst thing that ever happened to the Church' or, by contrast, 'a missed opportunity'. With the eyes of history, it would surely be an unwise person who could try to label the Council or the intervening half century in a single phrase or sound bite. With that in mind, I move onto my examination.

Sacrosanctum concilium – General principles of the liturgy

In looking at the significant points of SC, I am grateful to have been given this opportunity to read it again. Rather like the Highway Code, it is one thing knowing that you know it but it can be a refreshing experience to remind yourself of what you know, or bringing to your attention things you had forgotten or even not noticed before. The principles of the liturgy as outlined in articles 1–20 of the document are:

1. *The Twofold Action of the Glorification of God and the Sanctification of God's People*

God who calls us to worship is honoured and glorified; and we, his People, chosen and called, are made holy. We are called to avoid the dangers of a sense of 'it's all about God and me (as I ignore everybody around me)' and to avoid the liturgy being a presentation of our life and all that we are pleased to be able to say that we have done. This principle of the liturgy is demonstrated in this collect from the Eighteenth Sunday in Ordinary Time:

> Draw near to your servants, Lord,
> and answer their prayers with unceasing kindness,
> that, for those who glory in you as their Creator and guide,
> you may restore what you have created
> and keep safe what you have restored.
> Through our Lord Jesus Christ, your Son,
> who lives and reigns with you in the unity of the Holy Spirit,
> one God, for ever and ever.

2. *Liturgy as the Priestly Prayer of Jesus Christ*

Through the Mass, the sacraments, the divine office and the unfolding of the liturgical year, we are called to share in the prayer and the unique relationship of Jesus with the Father. This aspect of the liturgy is summed up in the words of a Sunday preface:

> For you so loved the world
> that in your mercy you sent us the Redeemer, to live like us in all things but sin,
> so that you might love in us what you loved in your Son,
> by whose obedience we have been restored to those gifts of yours
> that, by sinning, we had lost in disobedience.[1]

---

[1] Preface of the Sundays in Ordinary Time VII.

3. *Liturgical Prayer Is Trinitarian*

We can pray to or with any of the persons of God. But the model of prayer is a sharing in the perfect relationship of the trinity. This is so often seen in the opening prayers of the Mass, but perhaps brought out most clearly at the culmination for the Eucharistic prayer: the doxology and the Great Amen which should – where possible – always be sung: 'Through him, and with him, and in him, O God almighty Father, in the unity of the Holy Spirit, all glory and honour is yours, forever and ever – AMEN!'

4. *Liturgical Prayer Is Eschatological*

Our praise of God is rooted in the action of God in history, it is our present cause for thanksgiving, and importantly it is always led forward to the promise and hope of Heaven for those who are faithful. This principle is brought out in the words leading up to Holy Communion: 'As we await the blessed hope and the coming of our Saviour, Jesus Christ . . .'

5. *Liturgy Is Full, Conscious and Active Participation of All the Faithful*

This is their right and duty by reason of their baptism as outlined in SC 14. I have distinguished between these three words (full, conscious and active), to get to what they might mean in reality for the ordinary person. (1) Full: being there at the beginning and the end. (2) Conscious: making connections (e.g. bread – presented/consecrated/broken/given back to us in Holy Communion). (3) Active: knowing that the quality of worship depends on you as much as anybody else.

But misunderstandings of Sacrosanctum Concilium 14 might have created a greater gulf between 'doing' and 'actively being'. How often might a priest or somebody engaged in music, or reading, or distributing Holy Communion, or altar serving, or a catechist, look out at a Sunday congregation and ask: what are they doing to help? Why is it always left to the few to do everything? Well, first of all, let us not fool ourselves into thinking that the 'few' are all ready and willing to step aside if the sleeping giant were to awake and offer to take on some long-established roles in the life of the parish or worshipping community. But then, what does this principle of full, conscious and active participation ask of the average Mass-goer?

> To promote active participation, the people should be encouraged to take part by means of acclamations, responses, psalmody, antiphons, and songs, as well as by actions, gestures, and bodily attitudes. And at the proper times all should observe a reverent silence (SC 30).

Such participation by the Christian people as 'a chosen race, a royal priesthood, a holy nation, a redeemed people' (1 Pet. 2:9; cf. 2:4-5), is their right and duty by reason of their baptism (SC 14). I think it is helpful to consider for a moment your normal liturgical setting with a fresh view especially on SC 14. Whether it is here in Clifton Cathedral, or in a parish or chaplaincy. Maybe you are responsible for school or prison liturgy. Perhaps you are a catechist with responsibility for the Children's Liturgy of the Word, or even a church musician. Whoever you are, it is important to consider the principles for a balanced and uplifting celebration of God's praises, which are: glorification of God/sanctification of God's people; priestly prayer of Jesus Christ to the Father; Trinitarian prayer; future-orientated prayer; full, conscious, active participation.

A superficial judgement of people's engagement in the life of the Church – based on what they do at Mass – is selling short SC 14's vision of full, conscious and active participation, which is much more interested in knowledge of baptismal dignity, and of interior disposition to liturgical prayer, than what job they carry out on Sundays. That is not to say that outward engagement is not a sign of inward participation but it might be too simplistic to make such a judgement.

Full, conscious and active participation

SC 14 has long been held up as a pivotal article of the full document. What is full, conscious and active participation for the child who is beyond the age of Children's Liturgy of the Word and not yet an adult Catholic? What is that young person's level of participation – on any level – sandwiched between a high degree of engagement in their earlier years, and the thinking years associated with evaluating their faith and its place in their life, later on? And what is the full, conscious and active participation of the adult who attends Mass without fail each Sunday, but whose circumstances place them outside the Sacraments?

Recently I encountered a friend who spoke to me of her experience of Sunday Mass. She had never been married but had chosen to marry somebody who had been divorced and was not free to marry in the church. She made this choice and continued to attend Mass every Sunday, taking part as fully as she could but going now for a blessing rather than Holy Communion. She described the ill-feeling approach to the altar each week, knowing that she had made a life choice that had brought about this consequence of a blessing. But the worst Sunday for her came when, presenting herself at the altar, an extraordinary minister of Holy Communion extended a hand to her shoulder and said 'Thanks for coming today'!

It is breathtaking that a lifelong Catholic, wishing to continue participating at Sunday Mass, should feel so patronized by a minister presumably thinking that she would not know any different. She did not want thanks. She wanted something more, even by way of God's help for her week ahead. Those of us for whom the weekly or even more regular reception of Holy Communion can become so routine, might think again about how easy full, conscious and active participation is for us. These things require a broader view, because whatever the 'norm' might be for coming to Mass (having a sense of belonging, exercising ministries, and being a giver and a recipient of what the faith offers) young people and those outside the Sacraments are not the norm, but are still called to full, conscious and active participation, as a right and duty, by reason of their baptism.

What is full, conscious and active participation for the one-off guest at a baptism, wedding or funeral? Where no liturgical catechesis is available beforehand, no particular 'instinct' for the liturgy is present and it is at least possible that this experience might not be followed up very soon. Do we perhaps try to do too much in trying to make people's 'action' in the liturgy meaningful? Can the liturgy not speak for itself, to some extent, even for the passive recipient?

Summit and source/noble simplicity

In addition to the stated principles in SC 1–20, there are some celebrated phrases of the document that must be addressed. Chief among them is: 'The liturgy is the summit toward which the activity of the Church is directed; at the same time it is the source (font) from which all her power flows' (SC 10).

In the year 2000 Archbishop Vincent Nichols began his ministry in Birmingham with regional meetings with clergy, religious and lay people. At one such meeting, a priest asked him about the present situation and said, with some despondency, that we priests feel a little like petrol pump attendants: 'we stand at the pump Sunday after Sunday. People come, fill up spiritually and then go on their way for another week'. I remember thinking, is this going to be a moment for the Archbishop to share in the despondency? But he took the point and instead made it into a challenge for the clergy. To take the petrol pump analogy: if what we as priests make available to our people on a Sunday, and what we give of ourselves through preaching and presiding prayerfully, gives people a full tank with which to go and live their Christian life, making Christ present to their families, among their friends, and in their workplace? 'Then', the Archbishop suggested, 'I think I can live with being the petrol pump attendant'. For of course: 'One of the chief duties of Pastors . . . is to be a faithful dispenser of the mysteries of God' (SC 19).

He went on: if the alternative is the People of God being around the church all week and not evangelizing the various sectors of their life, I would much rather they filled up and left but returned the following week to fill up again at least!

The liturgy is the source (the nourishment, the inspiration, the Word of God to take with us) but it places a great emphasis on our personal prayer from one Sunday to the next – returning to the source, the summit, which becomes then the culmination and fulfilment of all that our week has been. Without becoming Pelagian about this (the heresy that suggests salvation by our own efforts), the very idea of the liturgy as summit and source only truly makes sense for the person who makes the liturgy a living reality and necessity – where summit and source are accessed regularly. The next article of the document that is as relevant today as it has ever been states: 'The rights should be distinguished by a noble simplicity; they should be short, clear, and unencumbered by useless repetitions; they should be within the people's powers of comprehension, and normally should not require much explanation' (SC 34).

How many times has an already overly 'wordy' liturgy become increasingly wordy as gestures are explained (sometimes needlessly, because the celebrant has misjudged his congregation)? Then the gestures have been limited in their dynamism to speak for themselves.

The Liturgical Movement

Fifty years on from SC, it would not be unreasonable to see this document and its effect on the Church's liturgy, as the start of a movement within the Catholic Church. To return to the wide of the mark prediction of Archbishop Grimshaw about English making its way into the liturgy, during Vatican II, it is as though some of the changes came out of the blue, with no warning, and that it could not have been expected. But what has become known as The Liturgical Movement had been leading to this moment for many years before. Across Europe, those who were versed in various disciplines of the Church's life became convinced that the role of the laity in the life of the Church was key to a 'Second Spring' in the Church. At a similar time to John Henry Newman's sentiments on an educated laity, others were looking to the public prayer of the Church as a point of access for the laity, and active participation within the context of public prayer was prophesied many years before SC. Newman had said:

> I want a laity, not rash in speech, not disputatious, but men who know their religion, who enter into it, who know just where they stand, who know what they hold and what they do not, who know their creed so well that they can give an account of it, who know so much of history that they can defend it.[2]

So, names associated with the Liturgical Movement are Benedictine monks Odo Casel in Germany, and Prosper Gueranger in France, and much closer to home, those who had a certain standing for their vision for the liturgy during the first half of the twentieth century, were perhaps appreciated more with hindsight, but often with suspicion for their progressive views on the liturgy. You will

---

[2]John Henry Newman, *Lectures on the Present Position of Catholics in England* (London: Burns and Lambert, 1851), pp. ix, 390.

forgive me the slight indulgence of mentioning, in this context, a priest of the Archdiocese of Birmingham, Msgr. James Dunlop Crichton – always a parish priest, never trusted to impart his views in a seminary. He died in 2001 in his early nineties. His writing was prolific, his wisdom on the liturgy both simple and profound. He and others, through organizations like the Society of St Gregory in this country, shared their thoughts on music and liturgy, and both before and since the Council, provided an important forum for enthusiasts and ordinary practitioners to grow in an appreciation of the liturgy and its place in bringing the Faithful to a deeper understanding of the life of the Church.

I think that the prophetic voices of the Liturgical Movement, and their paving the way for Vatican II, can be summed up in the writings of Romano Guardini, an Italian-born priest who spent many years in Germany, alongside others who shared the vision of a liturgy and a Church ever in the process of reform. Following on from the call for participation in the liturgy as far back as Pope Pius X, who in 1903 had first used the phrase 'active participation in the liturgy', it is said that Guardini is directly responsible for influencing Church documents of Pope Pius XII on the Church as the Mystical Body of Christ (1943) and the document on the liturgy, *Mediator Dei* (1947). These documents set the scene for what would come to greater profile in SC. Guardini wrote this, on the question of the relationship between the individual and the call to communal worship in the liturgy:

> When we pray on our own behalf only, we approach God from an entirely personal standpoint, precisely as we feel inclined or impelled to do according to our feelings and circumstances. That is our right, and the Church would be the last to wish to deprive us of it. Here we live our own life, and are as it were face to face with God. We are, however, not only individuals, but members of a community as well. In the liturgy we pray as members of the Church. Each one is bound to strive within himself, and to rise superior to self. Yet in so doing, he is not swallowed up by, and lost in, the majority; on the contrary, he becomes more independent, rich and versatile.[3]

---

[3]Romano Guardini, *The Spirit of the Liturgy* (New York: Crossroad, 1988). See especially Chapter 3: 'The Style of the Liturgy'.

A phrase that has its roots in the early centuries of the Church but which has guided the Liturgical Movement and many since is the Latin phrase: *Lex Orandi, Lex Credendi*. It is a phrase which simply means that prayer leads to belief. It is a strange order, and that is the point, because most people would automatically think of faith as coming first and prayer following as a consequence of faith.

Lex Orandi, Lex Credendi is the important insight that the liturgy is for some the first experience of faith (think especially of children – they come to know the actions and sights and sounds of the liturgy before they are able to formulate expressions of what they believe). But for so many more the liturgy can be evangelization, it can be catechesis, it can be prayer. In fact, the same liturgical celebration can work on each of those levels for different people. That is its dynamism. And those who saw the importance of the participation of the laity as a part of this saw that good liturgy strengthens faith.

The vision of Vatican II realized?

To ask the question: has the vision of *Sacrosanctum Concilium* been realized (yet) after 50 years? Or, at least, what is true now that was not possible 50 years ago? There are some notable advances. (1) Even more recently than 50 years ago, you might well recall that many marriages between Christians took place in sacristies and church porches – not quite under cover of darkness – but without fuss or ceremony, because both parties were not Catholic. That has changed. (2) The prohibition of entering other Christian churches, for Catholics has changed. Now, it is common for Christians to gather in each other's churches, acknowledging through liturgy and the Word of God a shared heritage. (3) In recent decades, it has become hugely significant to see popes accept invitations to visit synagogues and mosques – places of liturgy for their respective faith traditions. Most of all, the obvious celebration of the richness of the Old Testament Scriptures with members of the Jewish faith, not least the Psalms, which for us are the prayers on our lips that were known also to be on the lips of Jesus. (4) The RCIA (the Rite of Christian Initiation of Adults) has become active once more – something that has given us a real and life-giving understanding of the faith experience of the Early Church, and the process of coming to faith as joining a community more than just learning facts to become a Catholic.

But lest this examination sound too rosy let us not forget some of the ways in which the aspirations of Pope Paul VI and others have not quite made it. We can cite: (1) The number of people who still hunt high and low for a quick Sunday Mass without a note of music sung. (2) The wider selection of continuous Scripture readings at weekday Mass still so often being undone by the choice of readings reflecting saints of any rank. This is not necessarily an entirely negative point, if it means fostering a devotion to the saints, but it may mean the loss of something that could be such food for reflection, and which becomes so meaningless if not held together, from day to day, during the week. (3) Whatever happened to 'General Absolution'? There are many arguments for the norm being individual confession with individual absolution. Every priest would know the sacramental moments in individual confession which might not have happened in the most positive sense for people, had they not come and experienced individual confession. But surely the question can still be asked, what is it in the mindset of Catholics, about the quest for forgiveness, that will draw crowds to a celebration of the Sacrament of Reconciliation with General Absolution, but leaves churches on Saturday morning or evening with sparse numbers for individual confession? (4) In 1970, Pope Paul VI wrote the document *Laudis Canticum* launching the revised breviary, asking that the Divine Office be prayed by the faithful with their pastors. Where this happens – even in small numbers – it is an enriching experience, but I do not know how widespread it is.

Previous anniversaries of *Sacrosanctum concilium*: *Vicesimus Quintus Annus* (the twenty-fifth anniversary) and *Spiritus et Sponsa* (the fortieth)

I will continue with the theme of the People of God as a people of prayer. In the 50 years since SC, among the liturgical documents that have been written, two have looked specifically at progress since Vatican II, written as they were on the twenty-fifth and fortieth anniversaries of the liturgical Constitution. Twenty-five years on, Pope John Paul acknowledged that one of the barriers to the implementation of liturgical reform at Vatican II was the continuing preference for an individualism when approaching prayer; the idea of being part of something bigger, of my prayer being influenced by or shared with others, still being somewhat alien. This particular point was addressed head on by the Catholic Bishops' Conferences of England & Wales, Ireland, Scotland in their 1998 teaching document on the Eucharist:

> We are saved not as private or isolated individuals, but as a people, as a community, as a family. Salvation is, of course, a deeply personal gift from God: we are each called by name and are asked to respond in faith. Yet, "it has pleased God . . . to sanctify and save men and women not individually and without regard for what binds them together, but to set them up as a people who would acknowledge him in truth and serve him in holiness." To believe in God is to enter the "we" of the family of God.[4]

Pope John Paul picked up on the relationship between the need for both private prayer and liturgical prayer on the fortieth anniversary of SC when he wrote: 'Pastoral attention to the liturgy must instil a "taste for prayer"'.[5]

Without a doubt, something that was opened up by SC and has retained its potential in the Church's teaching to the present is found in articles 37–40 and pertains to cultural adaptation of the liturgy. In 2003, 40 years after the document, Pope John Paul wrote:

> The liturgical renewal that has taken place in recent decades has shown that it is possible to combine a body of norms that assure the identity and decorum of the Liturgy and leave room for the

---

[4]The Catholic Bishops' Conferences of England & Wales, Ireland, Scotland, *One Bread One Body: A Teaching Document on the Eucharist in the Life of the Church* (1998).
[5]Pope John Paul II, *Spiritus et Sponsa* (2003), 14.

creativity and adaptation that enable it to correspond closely
with the need to give expression to their respective situation and
culture of the various regions.[6]

Who could have been better placed to say so than the Pope who –
following the example of Pope Paul VI – had taken the Church
outside Rome, to the many cultures who embodied the liturgy and
reflected their life in their public prayer. As John Paul wrote in
Ecclesia de Eucharistia:

> I have been able to celebrate Holy Mass in chapels built along
> mountain paths, on lakeshores and seacoasts; I have celebrated
> it on altars built in stadiums and in city squares . . . This varied
> scenario of celebrations of the Eucharist has given me a powerful
> experience of its universal and, so to speak, cosmic character.
> Yes, cosmic! Because even when it is celebrated on the humble
> altar of a country church, the Eucharist is always in some way
> celebrated on the altar of the world.[7]

Many forget that while our staple diet is Sunday Mass, there is a
life of faith that is not touched for most people by Sunday Mass.
Maybe the pontificate of Pope John Paul did more, liturgically,
photographically, iconically, to make the Church's liturgy a positive
and life-changing experience across the nations of the earth than
we realize. The funeral of Pope John Paul II – a celebration of
public prayer – was the focus of the world in 2005. Similarly,
royal weddings and funerals have become a window on liturgy –
sometimes unfortunately, they have been arranged more for the
spectacle than for the integrity of the event, and have suffered as a
consequence.

So, to the present. I think that the Church's experience of the
revision of the Roman Missal in past months and years answers a
question about the impact of SC. The Church, in the 1960s, wished
for the Church's worship and prayer to become intertwined with
the lives of the faithful. It is beyond doubt that the debates and
concerns expressed over the new Missal have demonstrated how

---

[6]John Paul II, *Spiritus et Sponsa*, 15.
[7]Pope John Paul II's encyclical letter *Ecclesia de Eucharistia* (2003), 8.

much the Mass means to people, to what extent it belongs to them, and the degree of both fear and hope in terms of the outcome of revision.

I would assert that it is too soon to make any evaluation about the impact of the revision. It interests me that our reflections on the new Missal, comparisons between what we were expecting and what is now becoming more routine, comes now with the revision in place, rather than speaking of the 50 years since SC and still awaiting (with anticipation or dread) the reform of the reform.

The promulgation of the document Liturgiam Authenticam in 2001 signalled a change of direction in terms of liturgical translation. I had the privilege of attending some of the meetings of the International Commission on English in the Liturgy (ICEL), the body given the task of producing and English translation for the Roman Missal. I witnessed at first hand the expertise drawn from across the English-speaking world and the commitment that was given to the work. It is too big a discussion for this present essay, but it is enough to say that the Vatican intervention at that stage in 2001, while feeling very much like a break with tradition, has served in many ways to draw our new experience of the Mass into a more organic continuity with the liturgy of the past, earlier than we might have expected or felt we wanted. That explains the wrench from the past, but does not in itself mean that the end product will not serve its purpose as struggle with what is new becomes our prayer in the different circumstances of our life that we shall bring to personal prayer and to liturgical prayer. One thing that has been clear, and continues to be the case, is that anybody who suggests that the new translation has nothing to commend it is dangerously closed to being touched by (liturgical) prayer.

Music in the Church since Vatican II

Make no mistake about it: Vatican II expressed a desire for Latin to remain, and for Gregorian Chant to have a prominent place in the Church. Polyphony has not lost its place. But with the advent of the vernacular in the liturgy, this country has produced some excellent musical compositions. We have been influenced greatly by the liturgical music produced in America. In fact, in any given language, music has been inspired that has accompanied and enhanced prayer. Of course, there have been a few misguided ideas, but too many dismissive attitudes about Church music, dependent upon preference, taste and style have failed to respect the genuine contribution that music has made to post-conciliar liturgy. Perhaps the factors that need to be kept in view are: (1) The need always for music to be a humble servant of the liturgy and *not* vice versa. (2) The need for Church musicians to celebrate the creativity of others and not see them as a threat.

Church music, just like any music, represents different moments of our life and corresponds to memories. The tendency to always move forward and never look back can rob people of the liturgical memories that can be both precious and necessary to the journey of faith.

Where does the church go from here?

One of the documents given to the Church by Pope John Paul II, which is both moving and inspiring, was written at the beginning of 2001, at the end of the Jubilee Year, and cited the need to begin the new millennium still living with the Vision of the Second Vatican Council as our compass. It is called Novo Millennio Ineunte. As the new millennium began, Pope John Paul II asked the question: going forward, what is to be the approach we should take? This was his view:

> It is not therefore a matter of inventing a "new programme". The programme already exists: it is the plan found in the Gospel and in the living Tradition, it is the same as ever. Ultimately, it has its centre in Christ himself, who is to be known, loved and imitated, so that in him we may live the life of the Trinity, and with him transform history until its fulfilment in the heavenly Jerusalem. This is a programme which does not change with shifts of times and cultures, even though it takes account of time and culture for the sake of true dialogue and effective communication. This programme for all times is our programme for the Third Millennium.[8]

---

[8]Pope John Paul II's apostolic letter, *Novo Millennio Ineunte* (2001), 29.

Novo Millennio Ineunte went on to speak of the principles for continuing to keep in balance progress and tradition in the Church. This is his checklist, which contains no surprises, nothing new, as he says: holiness; prayer; the Sunday Eucharist; the sacrament of reconciliation; the primacy of grace; listening to the Word; proclaiming the Word.

In the same document, he draws us towards the face of Christ, which he calls 'a face to contemplate'. In every liturgical argument, discussion, planning session, reflection, there is something that we should never lose sight of: the person of Christ, the face of Christ, which is something different even from the words of faith that include body and blood, death and resurrection. All of which can, in their own way, take us into a language of faith that is life-giving, but does not speak of a personal encounter.

The liturgy – A bridge between earth and heaven

In contemplating the face of Christ the liturgy is forever an acknowledgement of the Christ who lived among us, the Christ who is now in glory. SC83 spoke of praying to the Divine Office in these wonderful terms: 'All who render this service are not only fulfilling a duty of the Church, but also are sharing in the greatest honour of Christ . . . for by offering these praises to God they are standing before God's throne'. This echoes the sentiments expressed in the catechism of the Catholic Church: 'To enter into the house of God, we must cross a threshold, which symbolizes passing from the world wounded by sin to the world of the new life to which all are called.'[9] Fifty years on from SC and mindful of Vatican II's emphasis on the Church and its place in the modern world, it is for us, the disciples of Christ today, our full, conscious and active participation which is transformed by the mystery and action of the liturgy, into a gift to be 'believed, celebrated and lived'.[10]

---

[9]*Catechism of the Catholic Church* (1993), 1186.
[10]Allusion to Pope Benedict XVI's apostolic letter *Sacramentum Caritatis* (2007).

6

Vatican II: On Celebrating Vatican II as Catholic and Ecumenical

Prof Paul D. Murray

Introduction

This chapter is in three main parts. The first part reflects on what it means to celebrate and mark the fiftieth anniversary of the Second Vatican Council, given the variety of ways it has been received into Catholic experience and the commensurate range of ways in which its significance has been interpreted. Here particular note will be taken of Pope Benedict XVI's call for a hermeneutic of Vatican II that combines emphasis on reform with emphasis on the continuity of Catholic tradition. Following this, in the light of current controversies about the Council's appropriate interpretation, the second part turns to asking more specifically after the Council's ecumenical teaching relative to its renewed emphasis on the catholicity of the Church. The argument is that far from the Council's remarkable articulation of a distinctively Catholic theology and practice of ecumenism being in tension with its understanding – commensurate with previous Catholic tradition – of the catholicity of the Church, the former is properly rooted in and flows from a recovered sense of the full implications of the latter. As such, Catholic ecumenism is here viewed as a means of properly restoring to Catholic thought and practice an expanded and full sense of the Church's authentic catholicity. The clear implication is that just as Vatican II, the most authoritative body of modern Catholic teaching, is authentically *both* Catholic *and* ecumenical, so should be contemporary Catholicism. Albeit in significantly changed circumstances, it remains vital that we return to the streams of life and renewal that the Vatican II documents represent so that under their inspiration our own thinking and practice can be deepened, challenged and refreshed in relation to our calling to bear Christ's 'light to the nations'. Drawing upon the Durham initiatives in Receptive Ecumenism, the closing section of the essay accordingly explores the practical implications of this at the international, regional and parochial levels of Catholic life and structure.

On celebrating the fiftieth anniversary of Vatican II: In service of the catholicity and unity of the Church

The Second Vatican Council, the fiftieth anniversary of which we are now in the process of celebrating, is widely regarded as the most significant religious event of the twentieth century; even more so in terms of its immediacy of effect than the 1910 Edinburgh World Missionary Conference that came retrospectively to be viewed as marking the birth of the modern ecumenical movement. Within Catholicism itself, it is undoubtedly the most significant event since the Council of Trent and the distinctively counter-Reformation expression of Catholicism Trent brought into being, which served to define early modern and modern Catholicism thereafter. Set against this backdrop, for the vast majority of Catholics now in their sixties and older, Vatican II was quite simply *the* defining Catholic experience of their lives, whether through enthusiastic embrace or aggrieved reaction.

In turn, for Catholics of my generation, literally the children of Vatican II, conceived and born while the Council was in process and reared in its aftermath, Vatican II has been the fundamental shaping factor in our experience of Catholicism, whether recognized as such or not. We are the generation who, at our most fortunate, benefitted from the waves of renewal and reignited enthusiasm for the living of adult Catholic life with confidence and imagination that was unleashed in the wake of the Council among many priests, the laity and religious educators, marked by a distinctive opening to the world and other traditions. This was experienced by many as the tangible resurgence of the life of the Spirit at the heart of the richness of Catholic life and tradition for which the prophetic Blessed Pope John XXIII had prayed in his surprise announcement of the Council in the Basilica of Saint Paul's Outside the Walls on 25 January 1959, at the formal closing ceremony for the Octave of Prayer for Christian Unity for that year.

In contrast, for Catholics a decade and more younger, there is typically a less tangible sense of Vatican II and its defining influence. It is background; relatively further distant, in terms of real emotional connection and constant reference, than had been the Second World War in my own formative years. What for older generations had been fresh about Vatican II and its aftermath has now become the received norm, lacking intrinsic interest and itself in need of refreshment and renewal. When joined with the intensification of secularism and the reactive postmodern impulse this can give to the clear defining and manifesting of identity, this perhaps explains the strong degree of interest among many committed young Catholics in their twenties and early thirties in the restoration of Latin and other more traditional expressions of Catholicism – to the occasional bafflement, it needs be acknowledged, of their parents and grandparents.

So, what are we doing in marking this anniversary of the Second Vatican Council? At the most straightforward we are making appropriate historical acknowledgement of the Council and providing opportunity to appreciate afresh its significance in a manner that can help transmit such appreciation to subsequent generations who have no direct connection with it. As with all 'golden anniversaries', the fiftieth anniversary of Vatican II is a good and fitting time to show such reverence and appreciation; and given that the Council took place in four sessions stretching from 1962 to 1965, we can look forward to 3 years of such anniversary celebrations. Indeed my entire adult Catholic life has been routinely punctuated by major Vatican II anniversaries: in 1985, while I was a 21-year-old undergraduate student of Theology, the Extraordinary Synod of Bishops marked the twentieth anniversary of the close of the Council; in 1988–89, while I was working in Adult Christian

Education within the Archdiocese of Liverpool, we held a series of public lectures marking the twenty-fifth anniversaries of various key documents; in his 2005 Christmas address to the Roman curia, shortly after the fortieth anniversary of the close of the Council, Pope Benedict XVI made his famous interjection on the hermeneutics of Vatican II.[1] I am getting exhausted celebrating anniversaries of Vatican II! If we were to celebrate each decade and each half-decade anniversary of Vatican II and allow each its full 3 years, it would only be rarely that we would not be celebrating Vatican II. But perhaps that is as it should be. As Yves Congar used to remind us, it typically takes over 100 years to receive a Council into the life of the Church.

For some this recurrent marking of Vatican II has something of the quality of mourning and protest about it: mourning for what they perceive as the eclipsing of the Vatican II agenda and the great work of the Spirit they take it to have represented; protest that things should be otherwise and a concern to preserve the freshness of Vatican II from slipping from view. This mood is captured by the title of one of Nicholas Lash's essays, 'Vatican II: Of Happy Memory – and Hope?'[2] Or as George Tavard, a *peritus* (invited theological expert) at the Council and founding consulter to the then-named Pontifical Secretariat for the Promotion of Christian Unity (later made a Council), recently put it with explicit reference to the Council's ecumenical teaching: 'The situation at the beginning of the twenty-first century shows that we have failed, even at the highest level, to exploit the insights of the Secretariat for Unity that were endorsed by the council.'[3] A similar anxiety is expressed by the *Vatican II: Voice of the Church* website that advertises in *The Tablet*.[4]

For others, however, this act of making memory has an explicit purpose of reinterpretation about it, guided by a sense of the

[1]See Pope Benedict XVI, 'A proper hermeneutic for the Second Vatican Council', in Matthew L. Lamb and Matthew Levering (eds), *Vatican II: Renewal within Tradition* (New York: Oxford University Press, 2008), pp. ix–xv.

[2]See Nicholas Lash, 'Vatican II: of happy memory – and hope?', in Austen Ivereigh (ed.), *Unfinished Journey: The Church 40 Years after Vatican II: Essays for John Wilkins* (New York and London: Continuum, 2003), pp. 13–31. Reprinted in Nicholas Lash, *Theology for Pilgrims* (London: Darton, Longman and Todd, 2008), pp. 227–39.

[3]George Tavard, *Vatican II and the Ecumenical Way* (Milwaukee, WI: Marquette University Press, 2006), p. 46.

[4]See http://www.vatican2voice.org/ [accessed 12 March 2013].

need to reclaim the Council both from extremely conservative denunciations of it as a fundamental distortion of Catholic tradition – a judgement associated with the followers of Archbishop Marcel Lefebvre – and from what are regarded as aberrant, incautiously progressivist developments of Vatican II. On each front the counter aim is to resituate the documents of Vatican II within previous articulations of Catholic tradition. This concern was already evident in the aforementioned 1985 Extraordinary Synod, over which the then Cardinal Joseph Ratzinger as Prefect of the Congregation for the Doctrine of the Faith (CDF) would have had significant influence. It is all the more explicitly so in his 2005 Christmas papal address to the Roman Curia, wherein the emphasis is very much on the need to interpret the Council as espousing reform within the continuity of the tradition.[5] In keeping with this agenda have been a number of practical initiatives also directed at emphasizing the continuity of pre-conciliar and post-conciliar Catholicism: the liberalization of permission to celebrate the pre-1962 rite; new translations for the ordinary form of the Eucharistic rite that seek to recapture something of the dignity and formality of the Latin originals regarded as having been insufficiently preserved in earlier vernacular translations; a string of statements from the CDF over past decades clarifying various aspects of post-conciliar ecclesial self-understanding.

This all poses a further question for us as to how we are to understand this range of responses to what is at issue in celebrating the anniversary of Vatican II. Why is the Church – which the Council's 'Dogmatic Constitution on the Church', *Lumen Gentium* (LG), describes as being 'like a sacrament . . . both of intimate union with God and of the unity of the whole human race' – why is this sacrament of unity not of one mind?[6] Why is the Catholic Church, which by definition is called to think 'according to the whole', shown to be thinking in discordant parts?[7] Here there are a number of points of which it is important to remind ourselves.

[5]See Pope Benedict XVI, 'A proper hermeneutic for the Second Vatican Council', x: 'It is precisely in this combination of continuity and discontinuity at different levels that the very nature of true reform consists', xiii; and 'In this process of innovation in continuity . . .'

[6]No text.

[7]'Catholic' derives from the Greek adverbial phrase *kath'holou*, literally 'according to the whole'.

First is that we need to avoid any idealized view of the Church as a perfectly integrated communion, free of all disagreement. A Church such as this has never existed – just look at the Acts of the Apostles and the stand-off between St Peter and St Paul, to name just one of the many deep ecclesial tensions shown to us in that book. Disagreement and tension are as normal in the experience of the Church as in that of society. Grace, the movement of the Spirit in the life of the Church, is not about the eradication of disagreement and tension in place of the achievement of a bland undifferentiated uniformity but about the Church being held, even deepened, in communion in and through such differences.

Second, as already alluded to, historical perspective reminds us that each of the great councils took a considerable period of time to be received into the agreed consciousness of the Church; in the process, generally provoking divergent perspectives ranging from enthusiastic promotion to hostile resistance and with subsequent reinterpretation and further development not uncommon. Think, for example, of the disputes following the Council of Nicaea, raging for over 80 years, between supporters of the *homoousion* phrase – 'of one being' – and supporters of the *homoiousion* phrase – 'of similar being'. According to Newman in his 1859 essay 'On Consulting the Faithful in Matters of Doctrine', for a period the majority of the bishops were opposed to the teaching of Nicaea on this point and it was only the pious practice of the laity that preserved what ultimately came to be reaffirmed as the orthodox Catholic faith, which is proclaimed each Sunday in reciting the Nicene-Constantinopolitan Creed.[8]

This last point is worthy of brief comment. Within Catholic tradition a very significant authoritative, magisterial teaching role is clearly accorded to the bishops of the Church in communion with the Pope as Bishop of Rome and assisted by the various curial dicasteries. But this does not mean and should not be taken as meaning that all forms of official teaching are equally authoritative or equally final. The Church is frequently still in the state of living through processes of discernment rather than having arrived at achieved stability and fixity. In such spaces of living through discernment, the laity and clergy alike have an essential role to play that goes well beyond mere passive acceptance.

---

[8]John Henry Newman, *On Consulting the Faithful in Matters of Doctrine*, John Coulson (ed.) (London: Sheed & Ward, 1961), pp. 109–18.

So we should take heart: if turbulence and cross-eddies are features of the Church's reception of Vatican II, it is because the ship of the Church is still in mid-stream, mid-crossing. We need remember that Christ is the one who has gone ahead of us calling us forwards; and that the Spirit, whose truth is always richer than any one narrow perspective, is the one who is with us, working through each of us – popes, bishops, priests, deacons, consecrated, and lay – to lead us forwards and to lead us deeper into the total truth of God in Christ. With this encouragement in mind, we turn our attention now to exploring the ecumenical teaching of Vatican II and what it means for us to seek to live the Catholic way of ecumenism that it represents.

On the Catholic ecumenical significance of Vatican II

While dichotomous contrasts between pre-conciliar and post-conciliar Catholicism can be unhelpfully overplayed, promoting the distorted polarities alluded to earlier, in the case of Catholic ecumenical attitudes and teaching it remains proper and necessary to remind ourselves of the contrast. Nicholas Lash remarks that: 'It is difficult for those who have grown up since the Council to appreciate how profoundly different, for better and for worse, is the *sensibility* of Catholicism today from that of the pre-conciliar Church.'[9] This is nowhere more truly so than in the case of ecumenism.[10]

The modern ecumenical movement has its origins in the nineteenth-century missionary activities of the Protestant churches and the performative contradiction this disclosed between the Gospel being proclaimed and the reality of Christianity's own multiple structural divisions and unreconciled differences. The impulse towards reconciliation and collaboration rather than competition in mission arose as the churches came to recognize

---

[9]See Nicholas Lash, 'What happened at Vatican II', in *Theology for Pilgrims* (London: Darton, Longman and Todd, 2008), pp. 240–48. Especially, p. 243.
[10]For further on what follows, see Paul D. Murray, 'Roman Catholicism and Ecumenism', in Lewis Ayres and Medi-Ann Volpe (eds), *The Oxford Companion to Catholicism* (Oxford: Oxford University Press, 2014/15).

the contradiction and the counter-witness it gave, leading to the aforementioned 1910 World Missionary Conference and related calls for a world conference also on matters of doctrine and order; between them representing the two sets of concerns – 'Life and Works' and 'Faith and Order' – that fed into the formation of the World Council of Churches in 1948.

While there had also been moves within Orthodoxy – through the Ecumenical Patriarch – to share in these initiatives from shortly after the devastation of the First World War, Catholic officialdom declined to participate. The 1917 Code of Canon Law forbade Catholics from sharing in meetings with other Christians (c.1325) and particularly so actively participating in or assisting with their rituals (c.1258). The logic was that the one true Church of Christ is to be straightforwardly and exclusively identified with the Catholic Church and that consequently all formal association with other Christians is to be rejected as a misguided irenicism suggesting a false equivalence. Unidirectional return to Rome was assumed to be the only authentic way forward, as in Pope Pius XI's 1928 encyclical *Mortalium Animos*, 'On Fostering Religious Union':

> There is only one way in which the unity of Christians may be fostered and that is by promoting the return to the one true Church of Christ of those who are separated from it; for from that one true Church they have in the past unhappily fallen away.[11]

There were, of course, some more positive notes also sounding, albeit less formally: most notably the work of the saintly Abbé Paul Couturier of Lyons, emphasizing the need for 'spiritual ecumenism' (i.e. the need to join in prayer with other Christians and so come to appreciate the living spiritual depths of one another's traditions) and refocusing Paul Watson's Catholic Octave of Prayer for Christian Unity into a more universal week of prayer for unity 'as Christ wishes and by the means which he desires'. Complementing this, at the level of ecumenically engaged Catholic scholarship and academic theology, the pre-eminent figure was the

[11]Pope Pius XI, *Mortalium Animos. Encyclical Letter on Fostering Religious Union* (6 January 1928) at: http://www.vatican.va/holy_father/pius_xi/encyclicals/documents/ hf_p-xi_enc_19280106_mortalium-animos_en.html [accessed 12 March 2013].

French Dominican, Yves Congar (1904–95) who, in spite of his years of official silencing during the mid-1950s in the light of Pope Pius XII's encyclical *Humani Generis*, came to exercise enormous influence as a *peritus* at Vatican II.[12] Indeed, even at the formal level the late 1940s and 1950s began to witness tentative Catholic openings, at least endorsing the value of ecumenical conversations and beginning to consider the possibility of Catholic observer status participation in ecumenical meetings. But even allowing for these and other such more positive ecumenical moves within pre-conciliar Catholicism, what actually flowed from the ecumenical orientation Blessed Pope John XXIII gave to the Council right from the outset in his January 1959 announcement of it – made, as earlier noted, in the context of the week of prayer for Christian unity – is quite remarkable.

The two key documents are the aforementioned 'Dogmatic Constitution on the Church', *Lumen Gentium* (LG), and 'The Decree on Ecumenism', *Unitatis Redintegratio* (UR), each issued in final form on 21 November 1964.[13] The contrast both of tone and content when compared with previous formal teaching could not be more clear.

For example, relinquishing the attitude of one-sided fault, Catholicism's own complicity in the historic breaks of the sixteenth century is acknowledged (UR 3). Even more significant is the clear recognition given that 'some and even very many of the significant elements and endowments which together go to build up and give life to the Church itself, can exist outside the visible boundaries of the Catholic Church' (UR 3; also LG 8). From this the implication is drawn: 'To the extent that these elements are found in other Christian communities, the one Church of Christ is effectively present in them' (UR 3).

Furthermore, these ecclesial elements are regarded as being of significance for the Catholic Church itself and not simply for the status of the other traditions: first in as much as the divisions prevent the Catholic Church 'from attaining the fullness

---

[12]Pope Pius XII, *Humani Generis. Concerning Some False Opinions Threatening to Undermine the Foundations of Catholic Doctrine* (12 August 1950) at: http://www.vatican.va/holy_father/pius_xii/encyclicals/documents/hf_p-xii_enc_12081950_humani-generis_en.html [accessed 13 March 2013].

[13]Also known as 'promulgation' of the text.

of catholicity proper to her' and so from expressing 'in actual life her full catholicity in all her bearings' (UR 4). Beyond this, it is even recognized that some of these ecclesial elements may have come to fuller flower in the other traditions than they have been able to do within Catholicism: 'anything wrought by the grace of the Holy Spirit in the hearts of our separated brethren can be a help to our own edification. Whatever is truly Christian is never contrary to what genuinely belongs to the faith; indeed, it can always bring a deeper realization of the mystery of Christ and the Church' (UR 4). Later Pope John Paul II would underline this in his remarkable 1995 encyclical on ecumenism, *Ut Unum Sint* (UUS), referring to other Christian communities as places 'where certain features of the Christian mystery have at times been more effectively emphasized'.[14]

These lines of understanding combine in *Unitatis Redintegratio* and *Lumen Gentium* with an emphasis on Catholicism's own need to learn, to be renewed, purified and even reformed. For example UR 6 speaks of ecumenism as a 'renewal' (*renovatio*) and a 'continual reformation' (*perennis reformation*) and, similarly, LG 8 speaks of the Church as being in a state of '*semper purificanda*', of always being purified. While communion with the Bishop of Rome continues here to be viewed as an essential aspect of the unity of the Church, this is no longer ecumenism conceived simply as a call to one-sided return but of growth on both sides and mutual journeying to a new relationship. Again in UR 4 we find, 'Their (Catholics) primary duty is to make a careful and honest appraisal of whatever needs to be done or renewed in the Catholic household itself'.

All of this in turn provides useful perspective within which to interpret the famous passage in LG 8 about the 'Church of Christ' subsisting in the Catholic Church. The first seven sections of LG, tracing an understanding of the place of the Church in the purview of creation and salvation history, speak not explicitly of the Catholic Church but of the 'Church of Christ'. Section 8 provides the first specific mention of the Catholic Church. In apparent contrast to the pre-conciliar statement of strict and exclusive identity between the Church of Christ and the Catholic Church, what we have here is: 'This Church (i.e. the Church of Christ) constituted and organized in the

---

[14]Pope John Paul II's encyclical *Ut Unum Sint. On Commitment to Ecumenism* (25 May 1995), pp. 14, 48.

world as a society, subsists in the Catholic Church . . .' (parentheses added). Quite apart from the linguistic awkwardness that would otherwise ensue, all the texts just reviewed clearly demonstrate that '*subsistit in*' cannot simply mean strict and exclusive identity – 'is' – given the full and repeated acknowledgement of there being real elements of the Church to be found outside of the Catholic Church.

Equally, nor is it cogent to claim that the degree of freshness introduced here amounts to a complete relinquishing of there being anything distinctive at all about the Catholic Church: all churches being equal subsistences of the one Church of Christ. Again the texts of LG and UR are quite clear that while there might be elements of the Church in the other traditions, something essential is also missing: 'our separated brethren, whether considered as individuals or as communities and churches, are not blessed with that unity which Jesus Christ wished to bestow on all those who through Him were born again into one body' (UR 3). Whereas, 'We believe that this unity subsists in the Catholic Church as something she can never lose' (UR 4).

Here, then, Catholicism is best understood as refreshing its self-understanding relative to other traditions in a way that both recognizes the dignity of those traditions and the real potential for appropriate Catholic learning from them while also continuing to maintain – as do, analogously, many other traditions in their own regard and in their own way – what Catholicism understands to be its own distinctive gifts. That is, in line with Pope Benedict XVI's approach to interpreting the Council documents as proposing 'reform in the continuity of the tradition', LG 8 can be interpreted as continuing, with Pope Pius XII's *Humani Generis* and his earlier *Mystici Christi Corporis*, to maintain that all the essential elements of the Church of Christ, including unity, are to be found in the Catholic Church alone, while also allowing for genuine freshness ('reform') through clear recognition of there nevertheless being real elements of the Church in other communities and churches from which Catholicism needs to learn and receive. In indicating this possible and cogent line of reading LG 8 in the context of this essay's exploration of Vatican II teaching on Church and ecumenism, the point is not to seek to bring final settlement to current debates; nor is it to claim that this is the maximum that Vatican II can legitimately be found to be maintaining in this regard. Rather it is to show that even a relatively cautious reading that observes Pope Benedict's hermeneutical principle is nevertheless required to recognize that Vatican II not only allows for but requires an appropriate orientation to receptive ecumenical learning on Catholicism's behalf.

In short, then, what we find within Vatican II teaching on Church and ecumenism, for all its concern to maintain deep continuity with abiding aspects of previous teaching, is clear recognition that Catholicism is itself engaged on a continuing story of reform, growth, and renewal and that in these regards it has much to learn from the particular flowerings of grace in the other traditions which can serve to enrich the catholicity of the Catholic Church itself.

This all links in interesting ways with *Lumen Gentium's* exploration of the unity and catholicity of the Catholic Church, even as it currently exists, not in terms of a strict uniformity but of a differentiated communion of local churches around the world, with differing cultures, customs and practices, in structural and sacramental communion with the Bishop of Rome (LG 13). This has significant implications for such matters as the effective, as distinct from merely affective, collegiality of the bishops with the Pope, the appropriate subsidiarity of the local churches, and the appropriate inculturation of Gospel and tradition within such local churches; all of these being issues into which Catholicism still has some way further to grow and to mature for the health, in the first instance, of Catholicism itself. In turn, by reading LG 13 in conjunction with UR 14–18, Avery Dulles finds here not simply a principle pertaining to legitimate and proper diversity within Catholicism as currently construed but one pertaining also to the 'reconciled diversity' that needs properly to be factored into any notion of the redeemed future unity of the Church *in toto*.[15] This brings us neatly to the question as to what it means today to live the Catholic ecumenical teaching of Vatican II?

Living into Vatican II's Catholic ecumenical vision

The formal entrance that Vatican II marked of Catholicism into the ecumenical movement opened a period of unprecedented activity,

---

[15]See Avery Dulles, *The Catholicity of the Church* (Oxford and New York: Oxford University Press, 1985), pp. 21–4.

achievement, and expectation, which many still look back to with nostalgia as the golden age of modern ecumenism. Starting with the Lutheran World Federation in 1965, the Catholic Church, through the offices of the Society for Promoting Christian Unity, embarked on a series of international bilateral dialogues aimed at promoting increased mutual understanding and seeking ways to overcome historic areas of disagreement. 1966 saw the inaugural annual meeting of a Joint Working Group with the WCC, followed, 2 years later, by full membership of the Faith and Order Commission. A sea-change had taken place at the highest levels and consequently promoted the assumption, clearly overly-optimistic in retrospect, that full structural and sacramental unity might be achievable within a generation.

In terms of the bilateral dialogues at least, the indications certainly seemed positive: through a combination of clarifying misunderstandings, exploring the fruits of recent scholarship, and considering differing theological frameworks as potentially complementary ways of articulating diverse facets of the one rich reality of Christian truth, one historic point of division after another seemed to render itself as no longer requiring to be viewed as communion-dividing. This is, perhaps, exemplified by the remarkable achievements of the Anglican-Roman Catholic International Commission (ARCIC) as ways were found through such historically divisive points as supposedly contrary understandings of Eucharistic presence, Eucharistic sacrifice, theologies of ordained priesthood, and even, during the subsequent second major phase of ARCIC's activity, the relationship between justification and sanctification. The latter anticipated by more than a decade the historic signing of the Joint Declaration on the Doctrine of Justification between the Lutheran World Federation and the Roman Catholic Church in 1999, effectively resolving, at the formal level at least, the central theological issue in the German Reformation.

Not all, however, was as positive as this might suggest. To take the Anglican–Roman Catholic context again, the high-profile status of the dialogue, the rate of progress apparently being achieved throughout its first phase of work, and a deliberate policy of promoting widespread local discussion of the dialogue documents and proposals as they emerged, all combined to promote intense expectation at the local level that became increasingly impatient with the slow pace of subsequent structural progress and, ultimately, lack of full endorsement at the formal level. While welcoming of what progress had been made, the CDF appeared in this perspective always to be identifying various further points of detail and interpretation on which sufficient clarity and identity of understanding had not yet been achieved.

Even within the ARCIC process itself, while real progress towards substantive resolution had indeed been made in relation to some key areas, in relation to others – most notably issues pertaining to the theology, structures, and practices of authority and decision making at universal and local levels – the limits of what could be achieved on the basis of an ARCIC-style dialogue process, at least as previously configured, came increasingly clearly into view. Although ARCIC II's 1999 document, *The Gift of Authority*, culminated in the remarkable – and, it needs to be noted, highly contentious – proposal that there could be an appropriate role for a shared universal primacy of the Bishop of Rome even prior to full communion, it was also clearly recognized that for any further substantive progress towards full communion it would now be necessary for each communion to engage positively with processes of change within their own respective traditions, in a manner exceeding what the erstwhile successful strategies of theological clarification and harmonization can alone achieve.[16]

Further compounding this sense of the bilateral dialogue process as previously pursued having now run its course, with the desired goal of full structural and sacramental communion being pushed correlatively further into the future, are the substantive fresh differences that have arisen between the traditions in relation to such matters as women's ordination and human sexuality.[17] These cannot be explained away as matters of mistaken understanding of one tradition by the other, or of complementary ways of articulating one and the same point; and regardless of what diversity of opinion there might be on the ground in relation to these matters in the respective traditions, it is clear that at the formal level there is, to say the least, not going to be any shared understanding and practice for the foreseeable future.

All of this has led some to believe that formal bilateral ecumenism in service of structural and sacramental unity is at a dead-end,

---

[16]See ARCIC II, *The Gift of Authority. Authority in the Church III* (1999), pp. 56–7, 60–2.

[17]Paul D. Murray, 'ARCIC III: recognising the need for an ecumenical gear-change', in *One in Christ*, 45, 3 (2011), pp. 200–11.

requiring a fundamental recalibration of ecumenical desire focussed only on the more modest goals of shared prayer, fellowship, and communion in mission. This places Catholicism in something of a jam: on the one hand the Catholic instinct is always going to be to strive for the full structural and sacramental unity – note, not uniformity – of the Church as a Gospel imperative, on the basis that no amount of shared prayer, fellowship and Christian action, vital though they all be, can repair the broken sign-value that we give to the world; on the other hand is the problem that the way ahead seems strewn with insurmountable obstacles and the approaches that have been formally effective, no longer so. The optimism that flowed from the opening of Catholicism to the ecumenical movement appears to have dissolved into talk of an 'ecumenical winter' and road-block.

At such points it is necessary to go back to basics and to remind ourselves of some fundamental truths of faith. First is that Christians are not actually called to be optimists: we are called to be people of hope, which is a quite different thing to optimism. Optimism is a form of reality-denial as we seek to reassure ourselves that things are really not as bad as they might seem and will all inevitably work out well in the end. Christian hope, by contrast, takes reality in all its starkness radically seriously, even into and through death, and knows that our role is not to be the architects and sole producers of a future that is not yet but its servants; that our role is to anticipate this future that is not yet but of which we can get glimpse and taste, and to ask ourselves what it means to live this anticipation now; what it means for us to be conformed to that which we glimpse and taste so that we can grow more fully into it; what it means for us to 'lean-into' the presence of the Spirit who is this sure foretaste and down-payment so that we can be held, set on our feet, impelled to action, called to conversion, and made living witnesses to this future in the here and now in ways that will both take us towards it and inspire others also so to travel. Second, with this, we need to discover a deeper, more radical trust in the overwhelming goodness of God, who does not drive us into corners in order to prod us with sticks: if the call to full structural and sacramental communion is a Gospel imperative, a constant, then so also will God's resourcing of the churches for this task be constant. The context and the challenges it entails might be different; previous strategies and resources might no longer be adequate, at least at this juncture; but fresh strategies and resources there most surely will be. Our task is to seek to discern them and to live them with courage, creativity, and fidelity.

In the previous section of this chapter it was noted that the central ecumenical contribution of Vatican II was not simply to open Catholicism to the ecumenical movement – which it obviously assuredly did, as witnessed to by the various subsequent initiatives indicated in the current section – but to present ecumenical engagement and Catholic ecumenical *learning* in particular as a means whereby Catholicism could itself hear the call to continuing conversion and renewal and so grow more fully into what is already the case. A number of factors and weighty precedents conspire to suggest that this basic principle now needs to be brought centre-stage and made the formal strategy for contemporary ecumenical activity.

One such precedent, already alluded to earlier, is the way in which ARCIC II's *Gift of Authority* drew to a close by identifying some remaining substantive issues for Anglicans and Catholics respectively to deal with; the implication being that any further progress would depend on such growth taking place precisely *within* the traditions themselves – as distinct from, in the first instance at least, *between* them. Another, in a more directly positive vein, is the way in which the 2006 document produced by the Joint International Commission for Dialogue between the World Methodist Council and the Roman Catholic Church, entitled *The Grace Given You in Christ: Catholics and Methodists Reflect Further on the Church*, explicitly focuses less on seeking to articulate a resolved agreed theology of the Church and more on seeking to identify the particular gifts that each tradition could fruitfully receive from the other in such a fashion as would both aid their respective flourishing and ease their path to future reconciliation.[18] By far the most significant precedent in this regard, however, is to be found in the quite remarkable sections of Pope John Paul II's aforementioned encyclical, *Ut Unum Sint*, wherein he extends an invitation to theologians and leaders of other Christian traditions to help re-imagine the way in which the papacy operates so that it might once again become the focus

---

[18]The Joint International Commission for Dialogue between the World Methodist Council and the Roman Catholic Church, *The Grace Given You in Christ: Catholics and Methodists Reflect Further on the Church. (The Seoul Report)* (2006).

for Christian unity rather than the continuing cause of division it currently is (UUS 95–6). Here we have clear, prophetic expression of the kind of imaginative commitment to the continuing conversion of one's own tradition that is required if the Christian churches are really to progress beyond friendship to the full catholicity of the one Church of Christ.

In recent years this basic approach has been formally developed and explicitly offered as a fresh strategy and way for contemporary ecumenism, referred to as Receptive Ecumenism; one that seeks to hold to and serve the traditional Faith and Order concern to work for the structural and sacramental unity of the churches, while also taking the changed challenges of our situation, as outlined earlier, seriously.[19]

At the heart of Receptive Ecumenism is the basic conviction that further substantial progress is indeed possible but only if a fundamental, counter-instinctual move is made away from traditions wishing that others could be more like themselves to instead each asking what they can and must learn, with dynamic integrity, from their respective others. As such, Receptive Ecumenism can be viewed as taking the call to growth and conversion that lies at the heart of the Gospel and applying it to the institutional, structural and formal ecclesial dimensions of Christian existence. In this perspective, each tradition is called to take responsibility for its own required learning rather than to wait on others to do likewise. The principle is that for all the many gifts in our respective traditions, we each variously fall short of the glory of God; that we each have difficulties, wounds even, that require healing. Much ecumenical engagement can be a matter of getting the 'best china' out: of wanting others to see us in our best possible light; one in which we do not even generally regard ourselves if we are honest. In contrast, Receptive Ecumenism is an ecumenism of the wounded hands: of being prepared to show our wounds to each other, knowing that we cannot save ourselves and asking the other to minister to us in our need. It forsakes the

---

[19]See Paul D. Murray (ed.), *Receptive Ecumenism and the Call to Catholic Learning: Exploring a Way for Contemporary Ecumenism* (Oxford: Oxford University Press, 2008); particularly Murray, 'Receptive Ecumenism and Catholic learning: establishing the agenda', pp. 5–25; and Paul D. Murray, 'Receptive Ecumenism and ecclesial learning: receiving gifts for our needs', in *Louvain Studies*, 33 (2008), pp. 30–45.

aspiration for a programmed step-by-step journey to a foreseeable destination and embraces instead a programme of conversion that will take each of us to a fresh place wherein new things become possible; but new places that involve each of us becoming more fully rather than less what we most deeply already are.

It is highly significant that the third major phase of the Anglican–Roman Catholic International Commission, ARCIC III, has explicitly embraced Receptive Ecumenism into its methodology as articulating a key mode in which it will work.[20] It is significant also that ARCIC III has been tasked with pursuing its work precisely in relation to the issues of authority and decision making at local and universal levels of the church that ARCIC II had come to see as now requiring substantive change on behalf of each of the traditions for further progress to be possible. For the Roman Catholic members of the Commission this will involve exploring how matters such as Papacy, collegiality, ecclesial subsidiarity and lay participation in decision-making can each be appropriately renewed, reformed and expanded in service of a fuller and deeper catholicity precisely through appropriate learning from Anglicanism. As to what Anglicanism might in turn fruitfully have to learn from Catholicism, that is for the Anglican members to ask and for the Catholic members to be prepared to help resource as desired and required.

Conclusion

This chapter started out with some extended reflections on what it means to celebrate the fiftieth anniversary of the Second Vatican Council in such a fashion as serves the catholicity of the Church – the call to think 'according to the whole' (*kath'holou*). In this context it was maintained that a concern for the integrity ('continuity') of the Catholic tradition of Vatican II requires also due appreciation for its appropriate freshness and renewal ('reform'). The central part of the chapter turned to explore the remarkable Catholic ecumenical teaching of the Council and, in particular, the place accorded there to the potential deepening and enrichment of Catholicism itself through such ecumenical engagement and learning. In the final part of the

---

[20]See   http://www.anglicancommunion.org/acns/news.cfm/2011/5/27/ACNS4874 [accessed 12 March 2013].

chapter a review of post-conciliar developments and achievements and their subsequent slowing led to a deeper appreciation of the contemporary significance of this Catholic ecumenical teaching of Vatican II, not only for Catholicism's own future health but for the furtherance of the ecumenical movement in *toto* in service of the churches coming one day to find themselves together in the total truth of Christ.

7

Vatican II on Muslims and Jews: The Council's Teachings on Other Religions

Prof Gavin D'Costa

Introduction

In recent years debate about the second Vatican Council has fallen into four camps. I'm grossly summarizing. The first, often associated with so-called 'liberals', bemoans the fact that the radical changes brought about by the Council have been left behind, ignored, and, sometimes, even reversed. The second, associated with 'traditionalists', mirrors the first. They too think that radical changes were made, but bemoan this. They argue that the Council had no authority to change tradition. The third group, often called 'conservatives', argue that the Council taught in continuity with the Church's traditions and anything 'radical' is a development, not a discontinuity, of doctrine. Finally, the fourth group are sadly those Catholics who are not aware of the Council.[1]

---

[1]For different narratives on the Council see 'liberal' renderings: Massimo Faggioli, *Vatican II. The Battle for Meaning* (New York: Paulist Press, 2012); Giuseppe Alberigo, *A Brief History of Vatican II* (New York: Orbis Books, 2006); John O'Malley, *What happened at Vatican II* (Massachusetts: Belknap Press of Harvard University Press, 2008). For a 'conservative' narrative, see: Matthew L. Lamb and Matthew Levering (eds), *Vatican II. Renewal within Tradition* (Oxford: Oxford University Press, 2008); Kenneth D. Whitehead (ed.), *After Forty Years: Vatican Council II's Diverse Legacy: Proceedings From the 28th Annual Convention of the Fellowship of Catholic Scholars, September 23–25, 2005, Charlotte, North Carolina* (Indiana: St Augustine's Press, 2007).

Here, in celebrating the Council's fiftieth anniversary, I will present a position that is a mixture of the first and third group. They are usually thought incompatible – which makes me a 'liberal conservative', possibly an oxymoron. I will argue that the Council did made dramatic and important changes in its teachings about other religions – and these are intended consequences and there can be no going back. I will also suggest that these changes, though radical, are not marked by discontinuity of doctrine. I shall focus specifically on Judaism and Islam to make this point. I will then argue that many of these changes have been misunderstood and therefore generated unintended consequences. Misunderstandings arise because they are not balanced alongside other teachings of the Council, namely on the religions. Employing such an eclectic approach has the danger of my losing support from either group. Most importantly, I believe this kind of 'eclectic' approach captures the actual teachings of the Council.

Some changes of teaching towards the Jews and Muslims

I want to focus first on some of the positive and radical changes brought about by the Council documents regarding Jews and Muslims. Inevitably, with the constraints of space, the complexity of the story is reduced.[2] The dramatic changes in relationship to both Judaism and Islam are found in *Lumen Gentium* 16, and its explication in The Declaration of the Church's Relationship to Non-Christian Religions, *Nostra Aetate* 3–4.

In the previous 'magisterial tradition', here understood as Council teachings or papal bulls and encyclicals, we find that Judaism and

---

[2]Besides the *Acta* of the Council, one of the best overall accounts related to the background and development of *Nostra Aetate* can be found in Giuseppe Alberigo (ed.) (1995, 1997, 2000, 2003, 2006 respectively), *History of Vatican II, Five Volumes* – English version edition: Joseph A. Komonchak (Maryknoll: Orbis); although *Lumen Gentium* 16 is not covered well in this collection. For the history and development of *LG* see Gérard Philips *L'Eglise et son mystère au IIe Concile du Vatican: histoire, texte et commentaire de la Constitution Lumen Gentium* (Paris: Desclee, 1967–68), 2 vols.

Islam are formally understood as heresies.[3] Why? For the simple reason that until the eighteenth and nineteenth centuries it was generally assumed in Catholic theology that: (a) Judaism embodied a wilful rejection of Jesus Christ; (b) and thus a wilful rejection of the promises of God made to the Jews, such that their covenant was abrogated or superseded; and (c) that the Jews were guilty of deicide. These assumptions meant the Jews should be classed as heretics: they knew the truth, but wilfully perverted it. Sadly and tragically we know the terrible potential and actual consequences of this type of theology: anti-Jewishness, which fed into the *Shoah*.[4]

Muslims did not fare much better theologically, but had more political and military power than the Jews. Theologically Muslims were understood to have drawn upon the Old and New Testaments and had perverted the truth of the Gospel. They too were guilty of heresy. The main theological attacks by Christians were on the Prophet Muhammad for changing and adapting this true tradition in the Qur'an to serve his own political ends.[5] In magisterial literature neither the Jews nor Muslims are classed as pagans, idolaters or schismatics, but as heretics. They knew the truth and had perverted it.

How could all of this change? The theological category of 'invincible ignorance' was absolutely crucial in generating a new picture and conception of the 'Jews' and the 'Muslims'. Its application to non-Christians has a long theological tradition but it

---

[3]For the history of Council teachings on 'other religions', see Francis A. Sullivan, *Salvation Outside the Church? Tracing the History of the Catholic Response* (London: Geoffrey Chapman, 1992), which includes all the major Council texts that are relevant. For a comprehensive tracing of magisterial teachings on Islam, see Andrew Unsworth, *A Historical and Textual-Critical Analysis of the Magisterial Documents of the Catholic Church on Islam: Toward a Hetero-Descriptive Account of Muslim Belief and Practice* (London: Heythrop College Ph.D. unpublished, 2007). I know of no single work that covers magisterial teachings on the Jews.

[4]See James Parkes, *The Conflict of the Church and Synagogue: a Study in the Origins of Anti-Semitism* (London: Soncino Press, 1934); and, useful although seriously overstated, Rosemary Radford Ruether, *Faith and Fratricide: The Theological Roots of Anti-Semitism* (New York: Seabury Press, 1980).

[5]See Norman Daniel, *Islam and the West: the Making of an Image* (Edinburgh: Edinburgh University Press, 1960) for a longer historic overview. Without overthrowing Daniel, a more complex picture is presented by Thomas E. Burman, *Reading the Qur'ān in Latin Christendom, 1140-1560* (Philadelphia: University of Pennsylvania Press, 2007).

enters the magisterial tradition in 1854 in Pius Pius IX's encyclical *Singulari Quadam*. It arose from a clear historical sensibility and frank acknowledgment that non-Christians were not necessarily non-Christians by virtue of their wilful rejection and perversion of the truth. This freed up the category of non-Christian so they could be emancipatory in different terms: positively acknowledging the truths they may hold and practice. This is precisely what shines through in the Council documents.[6] To briefly look at these positive statements let me first cite the key paragraph 16 of *Lumen Gentium*. I've lettered the sentences to be able to refer to them more easily:

LG 16: A. Finally, those who have not yet (*nondum*) received the Gospel are related (*ordinantur*) in various ways to the people of God (Cfr. St Thomas, *Summa Theol.* III, q. 8, a. 3, ad 1.)

---

[6]Of course, there were also other theological, political, social and personal factors generating the changed teachings at the Council. Despite the Shoah and the history of imperialism, there were virtually no calls prior to the Council to address the positive status of other religions. The issue was just not on the agenda. It came on to the radar through two distinct papal initiatives. In the case of the Jews, Pope John XXIII had been personally involved in saving Jewish lives in Hungary from his Turkish base. John was also friends to the French Jewish historian, Jules Isaac, who propounded the important thesis of 'the teaching of contempt'. In a well-documented meeting, Isaac pleaded with Pope John to reform the teaching that the Jews were guilty of deicide. Isaac argued this was the root of Christian anti-Jewishness. Isaac was clear: one could not change teachings related to the divinity of Christ, nor understanding him as the 'fulfilment' of God's plan. Pope John asked Cardinal Bea to draft a document on the Jews for the Council to remove the deicide charge against the Jews. Ironically, it was the report of the existence of this document, which had not been publicly debated at the Council, that created an international furore. The reaction in the Arab world was suspicious and critical. Many bishops in the Eastern Churches questioned the appropriateness of such a statement about the Jews given the political and military situation in Palestine. Pope John XXIII died and Pope Paul VI was left with the 'problem'. Paul visited the Holy Land prior to the document being discussed at the Council, and made a very memorable speech at Bethlehem, affirming the Church's deep spiritual connection with both Jews and Muslims. The wording of his speech was to enter the Council as the basis of *Lumen Gentium's* text on Islam. Paul was walking a tightrope in attempting to show both Jews and Muslims that the Council was not being partisan. Paul was also a member of a small prayer group, the Badaliya, which was dedicated to praying for Muslims. Paul had been deeply influenced by Louis Massignon's views on Islam. It is reported that Paul directed Cardinal Bea to make sure that every time the Jewish people were mentioned so were the Muslims. If it was not for the personal initiatives taken by these two popes we might not have had the positive statements on Judaism and Islam. If it was not for a statement on the Jews, there may have never been a statement on Muslims.

B. In the first place we must recall the people to whom the testament and the promises were given and from whom Christ was born according to the flesh. (Cf. Rom. 9:4-5) On account of their fathers this people remains most dear to God, for God does not repent of the gifts He makes nor of the calls He issues. (Cf. Rom. 1:28-29) But the plan of salvation also includes those who acknowledge the Creator. In the first place among these there are the Muslims, who, professing to hold the faith of Abraham, along with us adore the one and merciful God, who on the last day will judge mankind. Nor is God far distant from those who in shadows and images seek the unknown God, for it is He who gives to all men life and breath and all things, (Cf. Acts 17:25-28) and as Saviour wills that all men be saved. (Cf. 1 Tim. 2:4)

C. Those also can attain to salvation who through no fault of their own do not know the Gospel of Christ or His Church, yet sincerely seek God and moved by grace strive by their deeds to do His will as it is known to them through the dictates of conscience. (Cfr. Epist. S.S.C.S. Officii ad Archiep. Boston.: Denz. 3869-72.) Nor does Divine Providence deny the helps necessary for salvation to those who, without blame on their part, have not yet arrived at an explicit knowledge of God and with His grace strive to live a good life. Whatever good or truth is found among them is looked upon by the Church as a preparation for the Gospel. (Cfr. Eusebius Caes., Praeparatio Evangelica, 1, 1: PG 2128 AB.) She knows that it is given by Him who enlightens all men so that they may finally have life.

D. But often men, deceived by the Evil One, have become vain in their reasoning and have exchanged the truth of God for a lie, serving the creature rather than the Creator. (Cf Rom. 1:21, 25) Or some there are who, living and dying in this world without God, are exposed to final despair. Wherefore to promote the glory of God and procure the salvation of all of these, and mindful of the command of the Lord, "Preach the Gospel to every creature", (Mk. 16:16) the Church fosters the missions with care and attention

I will comment primarily on section B now; and A, C and D later.

Of the Jews, it is said that their election by God is never revoked because God never goes back on his gifts and his calling. The biblical dependence on Romans 9 and 11 indicates that this is based upon re-readings of Paul's letters. No longer can the Jews be viewed as deserted and accursed by God. But this also means that the Church has something to learn from the Jews about the ways of God. This section also indicates the Christian dependence, for its own existence, upon the Jewish people to whom the testament and promises were given. The Jewish roots of Christianity are emphasized as most foundational: in the flesh; Jesus is Jewish. These two points are monumental, although they may seem passé today. The Catholic Church commits itself, most seriously, to in effect repudiating the abrogation and supersessionist view of its relation to the Jews. (While these terms are not used in the document, I use them to indicate a difference between fulfilment and abrogation/supersessionism. I will argue below that the theme of fulfilment was never abrogated.)

We do not see an attempt to grapple with the question of deicide here because *Lumen Gentium* is devoted exclusively to indicating the positive doctrinal or theological elements that 'relate' these religions to the Church. The task of repudiating anti-Semitism was left to *Nostra Aetate*. The drafters of paragraph 16 were given one sentence to attend to each of these religions, so we cannot expect too much. But what we do have is deeply significant.

The next sentence turns to the Muslims and to the highest form of monotheism after Judaism. It is said of Muslims that 'they profess' to hold the faith of Abraham and 'along with us they worship the one merciful God' who 'will judge humanity' on the last day. Four important themes are packed in here which are developed in *Nostra Aetate*. First, Islam acknowledges the creator God and second, this creator God is also judge. Together these indicate the traditional pre-requisites required in Heb. 11:6: 'Now it is impossible to please God without faith, since anyone who comes to him must believe that he exists and rewards those who seek him'. Third, Muslims share a biblical heritage and in terms of 'typology' they hold the faith of Abraham. There was considerable debate about an earlier version of this phrase with objections to endorsing any Abrahamic lineage, precisely because in Islam, Abraham's son, Ishmael, not Isaac, plays the key part in Muslim tradition.[7] Hence the phrase 'they profess' indicates that Muslims understand themselves in this way, but the reference to Abraham as a typology of attitude is highly significant

---

[7] The first draft read: 'The sons of Ishmael, who recognize Abraham as their father and believe in the God of Abraham, are not unconnected with the revelation made to the patriarchs'.

in indicating a biblical lineage and typological connection. The *relatio* is insistent on keeping the reference to Abraham. Paul VI's Bethlehem speech had set a precedence. The fourth point is the remarkable phrase that 'along with us they worship the one merciful God'. It too is actually lifted from Paul VI's speech in Bethlehem.[8] It indicates that in the prayer and adoration of Muslims, they are united with Catholics who also worship this 'one God'.

In these compact two sentences, one on Jews and one on Muslims, we see a seismic shift of attitude towards these religions. Let me very briefly note a few additional points made in *Nostra Aetate* to indicate the energy and consequences, still unfolding today, contained in this seismic shift towards the religions.

Regarding the Jews there are three significant points. First, the Church is seen as 'spiritually united' with 'the descendants of Abraham'. Given the mention of Abraham in relationship to the Islam, we have the emergence of the notion of the 'Abrahamic religions' which has become so important in recent times. Second, in LG we found the word 'election' used. Now we have the words 'covenant' and 'revelation' used indicating the special *sui generis* status of the Jews. Again we find Romans being cited (9:4-5). Catholic Christians can never speak of the Jews as cursed or rejected by God. There is an axe put to this type of root of theological anti-Jewishness. Third, there is the repudiation of the deicide charge in all but name. Many fathers insisted that the New Testament indicated some Jewish complicity, so this was then balanced by stating that this responsibility could not be attributed to all Jews then or now, and that 'the Jews should not be represented as rejected by God or accursed, as if that follows from holy scripture.'

Of Islam there is a development of the four claims made in *Lumen Gentium* as well as the addition of three new lines of thought. The new lines: first, there is esteem for the moral life within Islam. There was serious debate and objection to the specific wording of the earlier draft affirming moral life in terms of the family because

---

[8]Paul VI's Bethlehem speech: those who profess monotheism and with us render religious worship to the one true God, the living and supreme God, the God of Abraham, the most high . . . May these peoples, adorers of the one God, also welcome our best wishes for peace in justice. And then later, in the encyclical: *Ecclesial Suam* (August 1964): 'Then we have those worshipers who adhere to another monotheistic conception (or form) of religion, especially the Muhammadans. Their true and evident worship of God merits our admiration'.

of the possibility of divorce within Islam.[9] Second, the importance of the Virgin Mary to Muslims indicates a shared heritage and spiritual practice. Third, there is clear acknowledgement of historic enmity between Christians and Muslims in the past, and the urging that both religions should move forward and strive towards mutual understanding and promote social justice, moral values and the peace and freedom for all peoples. This latter point was made specifically on the floor in relation to Christian freedoms in some Middle Eastern countries.

Since the Council there has been an outpouring of theological reflection and practices as the complex consequences of these positive teachings have been explored.[10] The Council opened the door to a genuine appreciation of God's activity within Judaism and Islam. These teachings provide genuine elements upon which to build good relations of learning, trust and respect and theological and spiritual exchange. As in all healthy theological discussion, theologians have explored almost every possibility, interestingly taking some of the Council's statements to their logical end, arguing that the Council's teachings generate a *telos* that means: (a) mission is inappropriate towards Judaism and/or Islam; and (b) that these religions can be means of salvation. I would call these the unintended consequences of the Council. Some unintended consequences are to be welcome as that is how history works, but I mean unintended here as they happened through a neglect of the whole context of the Council's teachings. In the remaining time I want to look at the Council's teachings and suggest that (a) (and, if I had the time here, also (b)) cannot be found in the Council. Of course, the debate inevitably

---

[9]The first draft read: 'Furthermore, as they worship God through prayer, almsgiving and fasting, so they seek to make the moral life – be it that of the individual or that of the family and society – conform to His Will', which was rendered as following in the final: 'Furthermore, as they worship God through prayer, almsgiving and fasting, and value the moral life'.

[10]Inevitably, many Jews and Muslims were disappointed for various reasons, as were some Catholics. Critics felt the statements either did not go far enough or avoided the most significant issues (such as a Catholic apology for its institutional role in anti-Jewishness, and the Muslim concern that there was not a single mention of the Prophet Muhammad or the Qur'an or hajj that were so central to Muslims). Personally, I understand these concerns, but think the Council went dramatically far and historically speaking, went as far it could have given the state of theological discussion. One has to remember that Councils are not research groups, but in the Catholic context, reflect growing consensus among theologians sometimes hundreds of years after the fire of the debate has burned most strongly!

spills forward to the post-conciliar Magisterium, but here I want to argue that the Council was against (a) on doctrinal grounds (and would also argue (b) on similar grounds).

The broader context of the Council's positive teachings on other religions: The necessity of mission to all peoples and religions

I wish to turn to sometimes forgotten teachings within the Council that contextualized the positive comments on other religions. Without these, the fullness of a Catholic approach is endangered. I will touch only on the following: (1) all religions will come to their completion through Christianity; (2) that the positive view of the religions assumes invincible ignorance on their part; (3) that all unbaptized humans live with the stain of original sin; (4) that mission is addressed to all of those who do not explicitly know Christ. Without these four teachings, the positive teachings alone misconstrue the Council. We need to return to *Lumen Gentium* 16 to pursue these qualifications to the positive teachings. I will focus on 16, sections A, C and D. Please see the quote above.

(1) All religions will come to their completion through Christianity

16A contains two key concepts that 'frame' the positive comments on the religions: *nondum* and *ordinantur.* The religions and non-religions described are classified as those 'who have not yet [*nondum*] accepted the gospel'. This frame means the religious adherents being denoted are addressed as *potential* Christians who are *not yet* (*nondum*) Christians. The *nondum* is explained by the term *ordinantur* (related) and the note to the sentence takes us to Aquinas' use of the word *ordinatur* in the *Summa Theologiae* III, q. 8, a. 3, ad. 1. Thomas is discussing the headship of Christ in relation to the Church and to all human persons. He is answering the objection that the unbaptized have no relation to the head as they are not part of the body (the Church). Thomas' answer resists such decapitation. He insists that Christ is related to all: 'Those who are unbaptized, though not actually in the Church, are in the Church potentially. And this potentiality is rooted in two things – first and principally, in the power of Christ, which is sufficient for the salvation of the whole human race; secondly, in free will.'[11] Aquinas employs Aristotelian terms here. 'Potentially' refers to something future, which at present exists only as a germ to be evolved. Hence, their religions are not being denoted as of actually being part of the People of God *per se*, but rather the positive elements being described lead them towards, relate them positively, *ordinantur*, to this actualization. This frame permits an unfettered positive description in 16B/C. Too often the first sentence is ignored in commentaries.[12]

(2) The positive view of the religions assumes invincible ignorance on their part

The other side of the frame, LG 16C is 'invincible ignorance'.[13] After depicting Jews, Muslims, and others who search for the unknown God in shadows and images, and non-theists of every kind, the doctrine of invincible ignorance is repeated twice. Why twice? Because the religions mentioned in 16B/C contain two basic classes of non-Christians: theists (Jews, Muslims and groping theists), and non-theists (all other religions, including atheists). Theists are referred to as those 'who are, without fault, ignorant [sine culpa ignorantes] of the Gospel of Christ and his Church' and non-theists are those 'who, without fault [sine culpa], have not

---

[11]See online *New Advent* translation; and also George Sabra, *Thomas Aquinas' Vision of the Church. Fundamentals of an Ecumenical Ecclesiology* (Mainz: Matthias-Grünewald-Verlag, 1987), pp. 156–80, who despite developing a very different interpretation to mine of Aquinas in general, is in agreement at this point about the manners of relating to the Church.

[12]As a typical example one might consult the commentary provided by Aloys Grillmeier, 'Commentary on the Dogmatic Constitution on the Church', Chapter's I & II in Herbert Vorgrimler et al. (eds), *Commentary on the Documents of Vatican II* (London, New York: Burns & Oates, Herder & Herder: 1967) [trans. Kevin Smyth from German 1966] who fails to mention this frame. Philips, Ibid., provides the only treatment of the matter that I could find. But he minimizes the point in his overall treatment of LG 16.

[13]One of the best treatments of this matter is to be found in Stephen Bullivant, 'Sine culpa? Vatican II and Inculpable Ignorance', in *Theological Studies*, 72 (2011), pp. 70–86. Bullivant is dependent on Sullivan's account which is thoughtfully challenged at various points in Ralph Martin, *Will Many Be Saved? What Vatican II Actually Teaches and Its Implications for the New Evangelization* (Grand Rapids: William B. Eerdmans, 2012).

yet [*nondum*] arrived at an express recognition of God'. The first expresses invincible ignorance in relation to Christ (the Trinity) and the Church, the second expresses invincible ignorance in relation to God. That the *nondum* is repeated from line one of LG 16 indicates that the basics of faith in God are still minimal requirements for the path to salvation. While there is a lack in basic theism, it is not quite as significant as the lack in non-theism. These two categories (theists and non-theists) cover the entire category of non-Christians treated in LG 16. Invincible ignorance is the presupposition of this positive view of these people and their religions (LG 16B-C) of the religions. Invincible ignorance is precisely what makes it possible to emancipate the religions and celebrate these positive elements.[14]

I would like to note an important irony. The earlier negative categorization of Jews and Muslims in the tradition became the very grounds for this positive view at Vatican II, as their true theism could now shine through unmuddied by their alleged rejection of and perversion of Christ. The mud of 'heresy' was washed clean by invincible ignorance: no personal and communal guilt at rejecting Christ could be attributed to Jews and Muslims *en masse*. A historical change of perception of these religions became possible and thus the development of positive doctrines about Jews and Muslims could happen. No earlier magisterial statement denies their theism. Herein lies the continuity.

In an interesting sense, the 'Jews' and 'Muslims' of Vatican II are discontinuous with the 'Jews' and 'Muslims' of the pre-modern tradition. The earlier assumption about their wilful perversion of truth, which is not a matter of doctrine but a prudential judgement about the level of knowledge that Jews and Muslims had of the Gospel, was now deemed inappropriate for a variety of reasons. Modern historical scholarship was one factor. Hence doctrines about 'Jews' and 'Muslims' at Vatican II operate with this curious discontinuity of referential identity from earlier teachings, which

---

[14]We see this same dynamic in relation to atheism. The Church in the Modern World, *Gaudium et Spes* 19, recognizes that 'invincible ignorance' even operates in a Christian culture. How? Because 'believers can have no small part in the rise of atheism, since by neglecting education in the faith, teaching false doctrine, or through defects in their own religious, moral, or social lives, they may be said rather more to conceal than reveal the true countenance of God and of religion'. This also allows *GS* to make discriminations about different forms of atheism (good and bad forms of atheism), but given the brevity and brief regarding other religions, this was not possible.

makes examining continuity of doctrine about Jews and Muslims particularly complex.

(3) All unbaptized humans live with the stain of original sin

LG 16D does not use the term original sin, but speaks of how theists and non-theists face Satan and self-deception. LG 14 has spoken about how Catholics have the most difficulties as they are confronted with the fullness of truth. LG 16D begins: 'More often (*at saepius*), however deceived by the evil one, people have gone astray in their thinking and exchanged the truth about God for a lie and served the creature rather than the creator (see Rom. 1:21 and 25), or living and dying in this world without God they are exposed to the extreme of despair.' Ralph Martin has written a fine monograph on 16D showing how this 'more often' qualification to the positive teachings has been almost systematically neglected in commentaries.[15] Martin also argues that the impact of this qualification and its citation of Rom. 1:21 and 25 is a reminder of Roman Catholic teaching regarding the effect of original sin.

Martin is also right in criticizing Karl Rahner's estimation of *Lumen Gentium* 16 as the most radical teaching of the entire Council in teaching 'salvation optimism'.[16] Martin does not suggest that LG 16 teaches 'salvation pessimism'. I would argue that the teachings on original sin on the one hand and God's justice and mercy on the other amounts to neither a salvation optimism or pessimism, but a radical 'don't knowism'. Martin's main argument is that mission should be emphasized relentlessly in the light of the Gospel.

(4) Mission is addressed to all those who do not explicitly know Christ

Let me turn to a fourth and most important factor that contextualizes these positive teachings on the religions. LG 16D ends with a resounding call to universal mission: to promote the glory of God and the salvation of all these people, the Church must 'Preach the gospel to the whole creation' (Mt 16:15). This was placed at the end

---

[15]See Ralph Martin, *Will Many Be Saved? What Vatican II Actually Teaches and Its Implications for the New Evangelization.*

[16]Martin, Ibid., pp. 93–128.

of paragraph 16 for two reasons: to indicate the necessity of mission to the religions addressed in 16; as well as forming the bridge to LG 17, which roots the universal mission in God's trinitarian missions of sending Son and Spirit 'in bringing to completion the actual design of God'.

The Decree on the Church's Missionary Activity (*Ad Gentes*) developed LG 17's theological rationale in AG 1–7.[17] There are two major points in AG relevant for my argument: to whom was mission addressed? And why? AG 6 answers the first question unambiguously and relates to LG 16, as the *relatio* indicates. This succinct definition of mission is important both for the groups specified, all non-Christians, and the groups excluded, all other trinitarian Christians:

The special undertaking by which the preachers of the gospel, sent by the church and going into the whole world, fulfil the task of preaching the Gospel and establishing the church among peoples or groups who do not yet believe in Christ [inter populous vel Coetus nondum in Christum], are commonly called "missions".

Two conclusions are clear. Mission is not directed towards other Christians, but is directed towards theists and non-theists. Theism alone is not enough to be excluded from the scope of mission, even if it is the first step towards salvific faith.[18] The goal of missionary

---

[17]See Suso Brechter, 'Decree on the Church's Missionary Activity', pp. 87–182, in Herbert Vrogrimler (ed.), *Commentary on the Documents of Vatican II*, vol. 4 (London, New York: Burns & Oates, Herder & Herder) [1967/1968, trans. Hilda Graer, W. J. O'Hara & Ronald Walls], 1969), p. 118. Basically and crudely, there were two groups: Schmidlin (influenced by Protestant missiology) that emphasized the proclamation of the gospel, salvation of souls, Christological and personalist themes and the canonists (e.g. P. Charles and A. Seumois) who emphasize implantation of churches, establishment of the hierarchy, native churches and focus mainly on ecclesiocentric and territorial issues. Both these thematics have long roots in the tradition. The final version of AG addressed a number of important points such as giving a strong theological rationale to missionary activity (AG 1–8), how it was different from other forms of missionary activity, defining the meaning of mission and missionaries, the role of different groups in the Church regarding this specific activity, and the territorial issues related to mission.

[18]This understanding is present in the 1350 code of Canon Law, 1350, s.2; and clearly restated in the revised 1983 code of canon law: 787 s.1: 'missionaries are to establish a sincere dialogue with those who do not believe in Christ'.

activity, also being attained by non-Roman Catholic Christian churches, is 'evangelisation and the establishing of the church among peoples and groups in whom it has not yet taken root'. Mission is clearly addressed to all those groups outlined in LG 16 as a doctrinal principle: theists and non-theists, regardless of the good and positive elements found in their religions and cultures, are united in their lack of knowledge about Christ.

There may well be complex prudential reasons why this universal mission may not be possible, but doctrinally it is an absolute requirement related to who God is and what God desires. Prudential reasons might include the legal restriction against preaching the Gospel in some territories (as is the case in some Islamic countries), or that preaching the Gospel in relation to a particular people may be equated by those people with the extinction of that people (as is the case in relation to some Jewish people). The single point I want to make here is that the principle of universal mission to both Judaism and Islam, as well as the other religions, is not only intact, but underscored by a theological rationale of some magnitude in the Council. Trinitarian missions are at stake, the very nature of God's life is called into question by denying this principle.

AG 7, after heated debate and serious and sustained criticisms of its original ordering, is a telling conclusion to the debate at the Council. It too sought to continue the commentary on LG 16-17. Speech after speech on the Council floor insisted that the truth of salvation outside the Church should not be highlighted in the first sentence.[19] It was not the case that this reality was being denied, but

---

[19]The Council did not overturn the traditional teaching of *Extra Ecclesiam Nulla Salus*, 'there is no salvation outside the Church.' In fact this teaching is reiterated three times, twice in *Lumen Gentium* (8, and 14) – alongside the other Dogmatic Constitutions, these are the most authoritative doctrinal documents of the Council; and once in *Ad Gentes* 7, precisely in its commentary on *Lumen Gentium* 16. And every mention of this doctrine also finds a qualification: it applies strictly, except to the invincibly ignorant. The actual interpretation of 'no salvation outside the Church' had been settled prior to the Council, back in 1947 when an American Jesuit, Leonard Feeney, along with his compatriots in another institution near here, had argued that no salvation outside the Church applied literally to anyone who died unbaptized as a Roman Catholic. The Holy Office, in their response, argued that no salvation outside the Church could *only* apply to those who knowingly rejected the truth of the gospel. It could not apply to those people who were invincibly ignorant of the gospel. This important application of invincible ignorance in relation to other religions had entered the magisterial canon in 1854 as already noted. The Holy

the fathers were arguing it should be stated only after categorically and unreservedly stating the necessity of mission.[20] Cardinal Bea, who was overall in charge of the drafting of *Nostra Aetate* was particularly concerned about the undermining of the universal missionary mandate. Eventually the ordering of AG 7 was changed because of this concern and I quote it to conclude this part of my argument:

This missionary activity derives its reason from the will of God, "who wishes all men to be saved and to come to the knowledge of the truth. For there is one God, and one mediator between God and men, Himself a man, Jesus Christ, who gave Himself as a ransom for all" (1 Tim. 2:45), "neither is there salvation in any other" (Acts 4:12). Therefore, all must be converted to Him, made known by the Church's preaching, and all must be incorporated into Him by baptism and into the Church which is His body. For Christ Himself "by stressing in express language the necessity of faith and baptism (cf. Mk 16:16; Jn 3:5), at the same time confirmed the necessity of the Church, into which men enter by baptism, as by a door. Therefore those men cannot be saved, who though aware that God, through Jesus Christ founded the Church as something necessary, still do not wish to enter into it, or to persevere in it."(Cf. LG 14) Therefore though God in ways known to Himself can lead those inculpably ignorant [*sine oerum culpa ignorantes*] of the Gospel to find that faith without which it is impossible to please Him (Heb. 11:6), yet a necessity lies upon the Church (1 Cor. 9:16), and at the same time a sacred duty, to preach the Gospel. And hence missionary activity today as always retains its power and necessity.

Eventually, AG 7 in this form received strong assent in the voting process. It insisted on the absolute necessity of mission to all those ignorant of the Gospel and that this missionary mandate founds its

Office argued that an implicit desire (*in voto*) for God through grace would suffice as the minimal condition for the possibility of salvation. However, the Holy Office did not stipulate precisely how this implicit desire might work and whether it alone was sufficient to attain the fullness of salvation. It left complex questions open as this debate was only just beginning.

[20]One of the best detailed accounts of the speeches and their interpretation on this matter is to be found in Francis F. Maliekal, 'Viis sibi notis. An Analysis of Ad Gentes 7a', in *Salesianum*, 54 (1992), pp. 705–41.

basis in Christ's explicit teachings and God's will. The theology of mission rooted in intra-trinitarian missions was left to theologians to develop further. And it stated the necessity of the Church as the means of salvation at the same time as acknowledging that this necessity could not mean a negative judgement on the eventual fate of those inculpably ignorant.

This balancing act carefully preserved in AG 7 is undone if one builds a theology of religions on removing the necessity of mission and the Church, just as it is undone if one builds a theology of religions purely on a literal insistence on the necessity of the Church. Certain liberal theologies have moved in the first direction just as Father Feeney back in the 1940s and the Society of Pius Xth has moved in the second direction.

Conclusion

I have tried to show that Vatican II is a remarkable balancing act. It makes a serious advance in Catholic affirmation and appreciation of Judaism and Islam – and there is no going back on this. The intended consequences of this move are still happily being explored and felt. At the same time it frames these positive teachings within the context of fulfilment, invincible ignorance, the prevalence of sin and the necessity of universal mission. The intended consequences of these latter teachings have failed to register as seriously in much Catholic theology of religions. If one emphasizes either of these two poles at the cost of the other, theological exploration goes awry. Tip the balance one way and you lose the rich spiritual doctrines and practices within Judaism and Islam, truths and practices that can call Catholics into question, and truths and practices that could deepen our understanding of the Trinity. Tip it the other way and you can lose the meaning of God's incarnation, his plan revealed in the Trinity, and the call to convert all peoples (not triumphalistically, but as servants and always with high regard to the patrimony of religious traditions).

Restoring this balance is part of the task of the retrieval of the Council. Catholics here can learn much from mission and evangelization among various non-Catholic sisters and brothers, especially those evangelicals who have not lost the missionary zeal that the Council had hoped to inspire.

8

Mary: Mother of God and a Model of a Pilgrim People

Prof Tina Beattie

'As Mary goes, so goes the Church'. This widely quoted saying is as true of Vatican II and the post-conciliar Church as it ever has been. From the beginning, theological reflection on the person of Christ ('Christology') has entailed speaking about Mary in order to ask what it means to say that Jesus Christ is fully human and fully divine – two natures in one person. As mother, Mary guarantees the humanity of Jesus. He was born of her flesh, his story belongs within the history of the human race, and he participates fully in our humanity. As virgin, she is the guarantor of Christ's divinity. Her virginity signifies that the conception of Christ constitutes a new creation, a cosmic event initiated by God which is outside all human power and initiative. The fourth century writer, Ephrem of Syria, beautifully expresses the mystery of the virginal motherhood of Mary in one of his Hymns on the Nativity:

A wonder is Your mother: The Lord entered her
and became a servant; He entered able to speak
and He became silent in her; He entered her thundering
and His voice grew silent; He entered Shepherd of all;
a lamb He became in her; He emerged bleating.

The womb of your mother overthrew the orders:
The Establisher of all entered a Rich One;

He emerged poor. He entered her a Lofty One;
He emerged humble. He entered her a Radiant One,
and He put on a despised hue and emerged.[1]

Equally important has been the quest to understand what is
meant in theological terms by the motherhood of the Church
(ecclesiology), and here too the role of Mary has been central to
entering into the mystery of the incarnation. The maternal Church
derives her identity from Eve who is described as 'mother of all the
living' in the Book of Genesis (Gen. 3:20), and from Mary who, as
the new Eve, is the first woman of the new creation in Christ, and
whose maternal body is sometimes compared in patristic writings
to the virgin earth from which the first Adam was created. From
this perspective, the Church belongs within the cosmic mystery of
Christ, occupying that paradoxical space between time and eternity,
heaven and earth, where the Kingdom of God is both now and not
yet, here among us and still to come. In the sacraments we have a
foretaste of the heavenly wedding feast – the *eschaton*, wherein we
enter into the fullness of joy that we experience only in transient
moments and epiphanies of grace in our journey through life.

The idea that Mary is a type of the Church finds its earliest
expression in the writings of Ambrose (339–397AD), who wrote
that Mary is:

> the type of the Church, which is also married but remains
> immaculate. The Virgin [Church] conceived us by the Holy Spirit
> and, as a virgin, gave birth to us without pain. And perhaps this
> is why holy Mary, married to one man [Joseph], is made fruitful
> by another [the Holy Spirit], to show that the individual churches
> are filled with the Spirit and with grace, even as they are united
> to the person of a temporal priest.[2]

It is therefore impossible to consider Mary in Vatican II outside the
context of Christology and ecclesiology. With that in mind, I turn

---

[1] K. E. McVey, *Ephrem the Syrian: Hymns* (New York, Mahwah: Paulist Press, 1989),
Hymns on the Nativity 11, 1 and 6–7, pp. 131–2.
[2] Ambrose, Exposition on Luke 2, 7, quoted in L. Gambero (1999), *Mary and the
Fathers of the Church*, trans. Thomas Buffer (San Francisco: Ignatius Press, 1999),
p. 198. For more on Mary in the early Church, see T. Beattie 'Mary in Patristic
Theology', in S. J. Boss (ed.), *Mary: The Complete Resource* (London, New York:
Continuum, Oxford University Press, 2007), pp. 75–105.

now to reflect on the representation of Mary in chapter 8 of the
Vatican II document *Lumen Gentium*, and I ask how this might
help us to approach the complex issues that arise regarding Mary's
place in the post-conciliar Church.[3] I want to suggest that if we can
understand the debates surrounding the person and role of Mary
in Vatican II, we might gain new insights into some of the difficult
and often painful issues that divide Catholics today concerning the
Council and its legacy. This has the potential to nurture a richer and
deeper incorporation of Vatican II into the life of the Church.

The Council and the Virgin

The place of Mary in relation to Christ and the Church was the most
closely contested of all the issues addressed by the Council, and
draft documents were subjected to repeated revisions. The debates
reflect a conflict between those who believed that Mary's unique
and privileged role in relation to Christ merited a separate document
dedicated to her (sometimes referred to as Marian maximalists),
and those who argued for a more biblically-focused approach,
sensitive to ecumenical concerns, which would integrate Mary into
the document on the Church (sometimes referred to as Marian
minimalists). For the former, Mary's role in the story of salvation
places her over and above all others in the Church. Immaculately
conceived and assumed into heaven, she is the Mother of God and
Mother of the Church, co-redemptrix and mediatrix with Christ,
whose glory cannot be compared to that of any other creature. For
the latter, her motherhood belongs within and not above that of
the Church, she occupies a pre-eminent position among the People
of God, and there is a need to avoid titles which suggest that she
plays an active role in our salvation in a way that would alienate
Protestant churches.

In the end, the Council decided, by a majority of 1,114 to 1,094,
to include Mary in the document on the Church, *Lumen Gentium*.
There are reports of some leaving the conciliar meeting in tears,

---

[3]There are a number of good studies on Mary in the Second Vatican Council. These
include: R. R. Gaillardetz, 'The Church in the Making: Lumen Gentium, Christus
Dominus, Orientalium Ecclesiarum' in the series *Rediscovering Vatican II* (Mahwah,
NJ: Paulist Press, 2006); G. H. Tavard, *The Thousand Faces of the Virgin Mary*
(Collegeville, MI: The Liturgical Press, 1996), especially chapter 12, 'Mary at Vatican
II', pp. 202–18.

saying that 'They have dethroned the Virgin'.[4] Although the title
'Mother of the Church' was dropped from the final document,
it was affirmed by Pope Paul VI in his closing address to the
third session of the Council in an attempt to unite the opposing
factions and restore a sense of unity. If we turn now to look at
Chapter 8 of *Lumen Gentium*, we can see how it tries to reconcile
these two conflicting views on where Mary belongs within the
Catholic understanding of incarnation, salvation, Christology and
ecclesiology.

The Virgin Mary in chapter eight of *Lumen Gentium*

The chapter is written in five parts and has the long title, 'The
Blessed Virgin Mary, Mother of God in the Mystery of Christ and
the Church'. Part I begins by affirming the role of Mary in the story
of salvation and the reverence we owe to her, in language which
evokes what we might call the 'high Mariology' of the pre-conciliar
tradition. As well as her motherhood of God and of the Redeemer,
the document refers to her as 'the beloved daughter of the Father
and the temple of the Holy Spirit', (*Lumen Gentium* 53) and as
'Queen of the universe' (LG 59). The 'gift of sublime grace' means
that 'she far surpasses all creatures, both in heaven and on earth',
even though as one of those who are to be saved she is 'hailed as
a pre-eminent and singular member of the Church, and as its type
and excellent exemplar in faith and charity' (LG 53). The document
goes on to stipulate that it does not offer a complete doctrine on
Mary, and leaves open questions that remain legitimate topics for
theological debate.

Part II offers a survey of Mary's role in the economy of
salvation, foreshadowed in the Old Testament and representing
woman's role in the story of the fall and redemption. It refers to
Mary's sinlessness, and insists that she was not passive but freely
cooperated in the work of salvation, in union with her Son –
'under Him and with Him' (LG 56). It affirms the doctrines of the

---

[4]B. D. de La Soujeole, OP, 'The Universal Call to Holiness', in M. L. Lamb and
M. Levering (eds), *Vatican II: Renewal Within Tradition, Part I. The Constitutions*
(Oxford: Oxford University Press, 2008), pp. 37–53, p. 48.

Immaculate Conception – the belief that Mary was conceived free from original sin[5] – promulgated by Pope Pius IX in 1854 in the Apostolic Constitution *Ineffabilis Deus*,[6] and of the Assumption – the belief that at the end of her life Mary was bodily assumed into heaven[7] – promulgated by Pope Pius XII in 1950 in the Apostolic Constitution *Munificentissimus Deus*.[8]

Part III considers Mary in relation to the Church, and here we see the emergence of a more restrained and biblically-focused ecclesiology which would set the tone for much post-conciliar theology. While avoiding the title 'Mother of the Church', it refers to Mary as 'our mother in the order of grace' (LG 61), having earlier described her as 'mother of Christ and mother of humankind, particularly of the faithful' (LG 54). She has an intercessory role in heaven which is part of her salvific role, she continues to watch over her Son's brothers and sisters with maternal care, and she is 'invoked by the Church under the titles of Advocate, Auxiliatrix, Adjutrix, and Mediatrix', which must be understood in such a way that 'it neither takes away from nor adds anything to the dignity and efficaciousness of Christ the one Mediator' (LG 62). In this, Mary is part of the 'manifold cooperation' of the faithful in the priesthood of Christ, the goodness of God and the 'unique mediation of the Redeemer' (LG 62). She is, in the words of St Ambrose, 'a type of the Church', and she is 'the new Eve' (LG 63). The Church imitates Mary in receiving the Word of God and becoming a mother who brings forth new life to those born by baptism, and like Mary she is

---

[5]This is sometimes confused with the doctrine of the Virgin Birth. The Immaculate Conception refers to the belief that Mary was sexually conceived by her parents – Anne and Joachim – but that she was preserved from the inheritance of original sin. The virgin birth refers to the belief that Jesus Christ was conceived by Mary by the power of the Holy Spirit, without sexual intercourse.

[6]Pope Pius IX, *Ineffabilis Deus – Apostolic Constitution defining the Dogma of the Immaculate Conception*, 8 December 1854, at http://www.papalencyclicals.net/Pius09/p9ineff.htm [accessed 12 March 2013].

[7]The Church leaves open the question as to whether Mary physically died before she was assumed, or was assumed prior to death. The Orthodox Church refers to this feast as the Dormition, a word which refers to Mary falling asleep at the end of her life.

[8]Pope Pius XII, *Munificentissimus Deus – Apostolic Constitution Defining the Dogma of the Assumption*, 1 November 1950, at http://www.vatican.va/holy_father/pius_xii/apost_constitutions/documents/hf_p-xii_apc_19501101_munificentissimus-deus_en.html [accessed 12 March 2013].

a virgin in the purity of her faith, hope and charity (LG 64). While Mary constitutes the perfection to which the Church is called, she also acts to call the faithful to Christ as the Church 'continually progresses in faith, hope and charity' (LG 65).

In Part IV, the document turns to consider the cult of the Blessed Virgin in the Church. As the Mother of God and as the one whom all generations call blessed, she is the focus of different forms of Marian piety approved by the Church, 'within the limits of sound and orthodox doctrine, according to the conditions of time and place' (LG 66). The cult of Mary is to be 'generously fostered', while 'gross exaggerations' and 'petty narrow-mindedness' are to be avoided (LG 67). To the consternation of its critics, the document makes no reference to popular Marian devotions such as the rosary, nor to the miracles, apparitions and pilgrimages that became such a feature of European Catholicism in the nineteenth and twentieth centuries – some would say as a way of expressing popular Catholic resistance to the spread of secular scientific rationalism.[9]

Finally, Part V affirms Mary as 'the image and beginning of the Church as it is to be perfected in the world to come' and as 'a sign of sure hope and solace to the People of God during its sojourn on earth' (LG 65). It points to those who honour Mary among 'the separated brethren' (LG 69), and calls upon her intercession for all people to be 'happily gathered together in peace and harmony into one People of God, for the glory of the Most Holy and Undivided Trinity' (LG 69).

A close reading of this short but immensely significant chapter of *Lumen Gentium* brings to light many of the delicate balances that the Council tried to maintain, and helps to explain some of the unresolved tensions which persist as we evaluate the legacy of Vatican II. Recent debate about that legacy has sometimes focused on whether the Council needs to be implemented in the context of a 'hermeneutic of continuity' or a 'hermeneutic of rupture'. In his Christmas address to the Curia in 2005,[10] Pope Benedict XVI

---

[9]See Barbara Corrado Pope 'Immaculate and Powerful: The Marian Revival in the Nineteenth Century', in Clarissa W. Atkinson, Constance H. Buchanan and Margaret R. Miles (eds), *Immaculate and Powerful: The Female in Sacred Image and Social Reality* (London: Crucible, 1987).

[10]Pope Benedict XVI, *Address of His Holiness Benedict XVI to the Roman Curia Offering Them His Christmas Greetings*, Thursday, 22 December 2005 at http://www.vatican.va/holy_father/benedict_xvi/speeches/2005/december/documents/hf_ben_xvi_spe_20051222_roman-curia_en.html [accessed 12 March 2013].

raised these questions of interpretation, arguing that since the time of Galileo modernity has presented the Church with challenges that require fidelity to the permanent, unchanging truths of faith and a willingness to adapt to take account of changing historical, political and scientific contingencies. This was what Vatican II sought to achieve. Pope Benedict said that, 'It is precisely in this combination of continuity and discontinuity at different levels that the very nature of true reform consists.' This is a helpful principle to bear in mind as we assess the role of Mary in the post-conciliar Church.

Mary and the Church after the Council

The immediate aftermath of the Council saw a sharp decline in Marian devotion. This might be partly because the embrace of modernity which the Council made possible discouraged many Catholics from practising an aspect of their faith that had always attracted the greatest hostility from Protestants and the greatest derision from rationalists. With hindsight it can be seen how *Lumen Gentium* might have contributed to that process. Although it affirms the uniqueness and glory of Mary's role and her active participation in the work of salvation, it is pervaded by a sense of caution and restraint, as if every affirmation has to be hedged round with a qualification in order to avoid offending non-Catholics. Some Marian feasts were dropped or demoted after the Council, and many influential Catholic theologians stopped referring to Mary at all, adopting a more Christocentric approach to theological questions.[11] All this contributed to the growing unease of those who believed that Vatican II had failed to uphold Mary's central role in the story of salvation and had thereby sacrificed too much of the mystical, maternal nature of the Church in favour of a misguided rationalizing and modernizing impulse.

This brings me to the other change that came about with the Council, and that is the shift from an ecclesiology expressed primarily in maternal imagery – Holy Mother Church – to a less mystical and more modern understanding of the Church as 'the pilgrim People of God'. When Pope John XXIII opened

---

[11]cf. Elizabeth A. Johnson, CSJ, 'Mary and Contemporary Christology: Rahner and Schillebeeckx', in *Eglise et Théologie*, 15 (1984), pp. 155–82.

the Council on 11 October 1962, he began his address with the words 'Gaudet Mater Ecclesia'[12] ('Mother Church rejoices'), but such language would soon be eclipsed by a very different idiom. John XXIII's 1961 encyclical, Mater et Magistra,[13] was rooted in the maternal ecclesiology that had been a constant feature of the Catholic tradition from the time of the early Church, but if we look at how the Church is portrayed in the 1965 Pastoral Constitution on the Church in the Modern World, Gaudium et Spes, we see how radically the Council had changed the identity of the People of God. For those who were eager for a more democratic and progressive Church, this abandonment of maternal ecclesiology was a sign of maturity and liberation. There was a sense that John XXIII's call to open the windows of the Church to let in the fresh air had allowed an invigorating breeze to blow away the cobwebs and create a bright and modern space for grown-up Catholics to inhabit. But for those who mourned the loss of the mystical, sacramental beauty of the pre-conciliar rites with their vast maternal potency, the sense of grief and loss intensified. The Council had not been a cleansing wind but a hurricane which had blown away the beloved family keepsakes and relics of an ancient tradition, leaving only a sterile liberalism and a reforming zeal in which the Church they knew and loved was barely recognizable at all.

Pope Paul VI and *Marialis Cultus*

As a response to some of these concerns, Pope Paul VI produced an Apostolic letter, *Marialis Cultus*, in 1974,[14] which sought to

---

[12]These were the opening words (in Latin) of Pope John XXIII's address at the start of the Second Vatican Council on 11 October 1962. The Latin text can be found at http://www.vatican.va/holy_father/john_xxiii/speeches/1962/documents/hf_j-xxiii_ spe_19621011_opening-council_lt.html. The English translation can be found at http://www.saint-mike.org/library/papal_library/johnxxiii/opening_speech_vaticanii.html [accessed 12 March 2013].

[13]Pope John XXIII, Mater et Magistra – Encyclical on Christianity and Social Progress, 15 May 1961 at http://www.vatican.va/holy_father/john_xxiii/encyclicals/documents/hf_j-xxiii_enc_15051961_mater_en.html [accessed 12 March 2013].

[14]Pope Paul VI, Marialis Cultus – Apostolic Exhortation for the Right Ordering and Development of Devotion to the Blessed Virgin Mary, 2 February 1974, at http://www.vatican.va/holy_father/paul_vi/apost_exhortations/documents/hf_p-vi_exh_19740202_marialis-cultus_en.html [accessed 12 March 2013].

redress the imbalance and restore Marian devotion to its rightful place. Many regard this as one of the finest modern documents on Mary. It affirms the significance of Marian feasts, commemorations and local devotions for the liturgical life of the Church, and it criticizes both those who were too quick to suppress Marian devotions, and those who accorded them too much prominence, for example by incorporating them into the celebration of the Mass. We see in *Marialis Cultus* signs of the continuing conflict between those who had struggled so intensely over the role of the Virgin during the Council itself. Pope Paul VI also acknowledges the difficulty that some forms of Marian devotion present for modern women, who may not find it easy to reconcile their own increasing opportunities for equality and participation with what may seem like the restricted horizons of the life of Mary of Nazareth. He offers a potent affirmation of Mary's strength and courage, and her example as a perfect model of 'the disciple who works for that justice which sets free the oppressed and for that charity which assists the needy; but above all, the disciple who is the active witness of that love which builds up Christ in people's hearts' (MC 37).

This weaving together of traditional pieties and devotions with contemporary concerns for social justice and the role of women reflects the vibrant theological context of Catholicism in the early 1970s, which saw the emergence of a variety of contextual, liberationist and feminist theologies. Mary was often relatively marginal to these theological perspectives, and when she did appear, it tended to be more in the guise of an emancipatory political figure or liberating role model than as the Holy Mother of God. Perhaps the most creative attempt to offer a Marian theology that combined both these elements was a book by Brazilian feminist theologians Ivone Gebara and María Clara Bingemer, *Mary, Mother of God, Mother of the Poor.* They speak of Mary as a mystery who:

> brings a new word about the world, about this world where men and women are born, grow, love, suffer, live, clash, rejoice, and die. . . . The mystery of Mary says that the world is not just a sinister stage for an absurd tragedy where victors and vanquished are ever the same, but a place where those who fight the good fight of life can hope for victory, under the merciful

eyes of the Mother of Life. Their victory is guaranteed in her who is victorious in God, but who does not abandon those who acknowledge her and call on her as advocate and mother.[15]

Such attempts to bring liberationist and feminist perspectives to Marian theology without losing the essential mystery and holiness of Mary's role in the story of salvation were overshadowed by different theological perspectives and emphases which emerged during the long papacy of Pope John Paul II. Gradually, the grassroots approach which had been a feature of post-conciliar theology and magisterial teaching began to be replaced by a more top-down approach, symptomatic of an increasingly authoritarian attitude to questions of Church teaching and discipline, and manifesting a quest to reclaim some of the more traditional and mystical aspects of the pre-conciliar church. A significant influence on these theological developments was Swiss theologian Hans Urs von Balthasar, who was a vocal critic of the Council and whose theology was much admired by John Paul II. If Karl Rahner had been 'the Holy Ghost' of Vatican II as some suggested, his vociferous opponent von Balthasar came into his own in the 1980s, and today it is von Balthasar rather than Rahner who is the theologian of choice in many seminaries and Catholic universities.

Theology of the body and nuptial ecclesiology

Von Balthasar lamented what he saw as the loss of the mystical, Marian character of the Church after the Council. In typically effulgent language, he complained that it had become:

> more than ever a male Church, if perhaps one should not say a sexless entity, in which woman may gain for herself a place to the extent that she is ready herself to become such an entity.... What can one say of "political theology" and of "critical Catholicism"? They are outlines for discussion for professors of theology and anti-repressive students, but scarcely for a congregation which

---

[15]Ivone Gebara and María Clara Bingemer, *Mary, Mother of God, Mother of the Poor* (Tunbridge Wells: Burns & Oates, 1989), p. 174.

still consists of children, women, old men, and the sick . . . May the reason for the domination of such typically male and abstract notions be because of the abandonment of the deep femininity of the marian character of the Church?[16]

Under von Balthasar's influence, there is today renewed theological interest in the Marian Church. This is closely associated with John Paul II's theology of the body, which he developed in a series of general audiences on the Book of Genesis between 1979 and 1984.[17] The vision of human sexuality that he presented during these audiences has become the focus of a widespread theological movement, particularly in the United States.[18] Rejecting the more progressive and liberalizing trends of the Council, and hostile to secular feminism, this Theology of the Body movement calls for 'a new feminism' which celebrates the 'feminine genius' of women – both terms used by John Paul II. Its main supporters are educated Western Catholics, and it remains an open question as to how far it is capable of adequately addressing issues of motherhood, poverty and family relationships for poorer communities or for those who are alienated by what can seem like stereotypical and romanticized representations of maternal femininity.

Such ideas also reflect a changing ecclesiology, for they introduce yet another new perspective into the traditional understanding of the nature of the Church. This has come about through an almost exclusive emphasis on the nuptial relationship between the Church as Bride represented by all the faithful as the body of Christ, and Christ the Bridegroom as the Head, represented by the priest.[19] Although there has always been a nuptial dimension to ecclesiology,

---

[16]Hans Urs von Balthasar, *Elucidations*, trans. John Riches (London: SPCK, 1975), p. 70. It is interesting that von Balthasar groups women with children, old men, and the sick, over and against professors of theology. Professors of theology include an abundance of old men and even a few women.

[17]See Pope John Paul II, *Original Unity of Man and Woman: 'Catechesis on the Book of Genesis'* (1979–80) at http://www.vatican.va/holy_father/john_paul_ii/audiences/catechesis_genesis/index.htm [accessed 12 March 2013].

[18]See the website 'Theology of the Body.net' at http://www.theologyofthebody.net/ [accessed 12 March 2013].

[19]For more on this, see Fergus Kerr, *Twentieth-Century Catholic Theologians* (Oxford: Blackwell Publishing, 2007), chs 8–12. This book is a lucid and often highly entertaining introduction to all the great Catholic theologians of the twentieth century, and a valuable guide for understanding the theological context surrounding Vatican II and its aftermath.

today it sometimes comes close to sexual literalism (again under von Balthasar's influence) in such a way that the Mass comes to be represented as an act of sexual consummation between a feminized creation and an essentially masculine Christ – an ecclesiology which owes more to pagan mythology than to Christian tradition, and which becomes disconcertingly pre-oedipal if applied to the relationship between Mary and Christ. The underlying rationale is the need to justify the exclusive masculinity of the priesthood, but it also serves to reinforce traditional domestic roles and sexual identities at a time of accelerating social and cultural change.

Yet it would be wrong to see all this only in terms of conservative or reactionary tendencies within the Church. There is widespread recognition today that the Council did indeed sacrifice too much of the sacramental mystery and transcendence of the pre-conciliar Church. Charlene Spretnak is an American feminist writer at the opposite end of the theological spectrum from von Balthasar, but in her book *Missing Mary* she appeals for a rediscovery of the Catholic Church as 'a container and guardian of mysteries far greater than itself'. She describes what she sees as the destructive influence of rationalizing modernity on Catholic devotion:

> When...the Roman Catholic Church deemphasized and banished an essential cluster of (Marian) spiritual mysteries, as well as the evocative expression of ritual and symbol that had grown around them, a profound loss ensued. Today, the theology and liturgy of the Catholic Church is less "cluttered," less mystical, and less comprehensive in its spiritual scope. Its tight, clear focus is far more "rational" but far less whole. We who once partook of a vast spiritual banquet with boundaries beyond our ken are now allotted spare rations, culled by the blades of a "rationalized" agenda more acceptable to the modern mindset.[20]

These changes can be traced back to the documents of Vatican II, and most particularly to *Lumen Gentium*. In its attempt to articulate an ecclesiology and a corresponding Mariology that would find widespread acceptance among Christians and would provide a creative forum for ecumenical dialogue, *Lumen Gentium*

---

[20]Charlene Spretnak, *Missing Mary: The Queen of Heaven and Her Re-Emergence in the Modern Church* (New York: Palgrave Macmillan, 2004), p. 4.

may have sacrificed too much that was distinctively Catholic and deeply valued by many across the Catholic spectrum. As part of the ongoing task of embodying the Council within the life of the Church through a process of discernment and adaptation, we must ask how a recovery of the Marian tradition might inspire a renewed appreciation of the grace which suffuses all creation with God's love and endows all nature with sacramental significance. Only then will Catholic faith and devotion be suffused with an incarnational awareness of the mystery that we discover in the paradoxical union between Word and flesh, heaven and earth, creator and creation, in the person of Jesus Christ. So is it possible to discern a way forward which might lead us beyond some of the polarities and conflicts which are such a feature of Catholic life today, to a more holistic and integrated appreciation of Mary's place in the mystery of Christ and the Church, in the context of the post-conciliar era? That is the question which informs the last part of this reflection.

Repairing the sacred canopy

The sociologist Peter Berger wrote an influential book called *The Sacred Canopy* in the 1960s, in which he spoke about the need to understand the role that religions play in weaving human beings into a cosmic vision.[21] In Catholic Christianity, this sacred canopy is the sacramental tradition, by way of which the Christian belief that creator and creation are brought into a redeemed and transformed relationship in Jesus Christ is embodied in the everyday lives of believers throughout the ages. This is sometimes referred to as 'the sacramental imagination', which is our way of being in the world as a hopeful and loving response to the grace of God that suffuses and sustains everything that exists. This requires prayerful attentiveness to the wonder that we experience when we are able, in the words of William Blake, 'To see a world in a grain of sand, And a heaven in a wild flower'.

But Berger also warns that the symbolic worlds we inhabit can become coercive and oppressive if they are imposed on us in such a way that we are no longer able to internalize their meanings so

---

[21]Peter Berger, *The Sacred Canopy: Elements of a Sociological Theory of Religion* (New York: Open Road – Integrated Media, 2011).

that they become part of who we are. The restoration of the Latin rite and the imposition of the new translation of the liturgy with its archaic and obtuse terminology can be seen as an attempt at restoration, but one cannot reawaken the sacramental imagination by force, nor by a return to devotions and rites that seem alien to many modern Catholics. For many Catholics today, the crucial sense of connectedness between the symbolic and sacramental life of faith and the inner values and meanings we give to our lives has become strained to breaking point. Only if we can rediscover a space of fluidity and interaction between the real experiences of people's lives with all their messy contradictions and confusions, and the unfolding mysteries of the sacramental tradition with its eschatological promise of a reconciled creation, can there be a renewed sense of expressive reality and profound contemplation in the liturgical life of faith.

If we are to repair the torn canopy of the Catholic mystical and sacramental tradition, we need to do so in a spirit of liturgical playfulness, in the way that children discover the wonder of the world through imaginative freedom and creativity, but also through intense concentration and absorption in the here and now. Play is kissed by infinity because, whether it involves creating a work of art, playing a piece of music, relaxing among friends or entering into the mystery of the liturgy, it transports us into an altered state of consciousness within which our sense of time and space is dissolved, our rational mind loses its grip on our senses and feelings, and we become aware of the presence of God as an irresistible mystery beckoning to us within and beyond the horizons of the known and knowable world.

Modern psychology tells us that the maternal relationship remains the imagined space of creativity and play throughout our adult lives. The infant relationship to the mother shapes our unconscious world and has the potential to open our souls to different ways of being. Such insights invite the Catholic Church to rediscover the immense potential of the Marian tradition and the maternal Church, but this must avoid becoming a regressive move away from the challenges of the modern world into an infantilizing maternal comfort zone presided over by an authoritarian patriarchal hierarchy. A Marian revival needs to learn from psychoanalysis, it needs to incorporate the experiences and insights of mothers themselves, and it needs to draw on the work of many women philosophers and theologians who write on motherhood and maternal ethics, in order better to understand the riches yet to be discovered in this maternal tradition.

The environmental crisis has made us aware of the canopy of the rainforest as a vast overarching source of life and nourishment for the abundance of life forms that flourish within and beneath it, while it oxygenates and sustains our beautiful planet in ways that affect the lives of every living creature on earth. The Church is God's sacred canopy over creation, and it too has sustained and nurtured many, many forms of life and ways of being, not only among Catholics but also among many who live far beyond its physical boundaries. In his opening address to the Council, John XXIII quoted St Cyprian who, writing in the third century, said that:

> The Church, radiant with the light of her Lord, sheds her rays over all the world, and that light of hers remains one, though everywhere diffused; her corporate unity is not divided. She spreads her luxuriant branches over all the earth; she sends out her fair-flowing streams ever farther afield. But the head is one; the source is one. She is the one mother of countless generations. And we are her children, born of her, fed with her milk, animated with her breath.

The question today is whether this sacred canopy can once again become a space capable of sustaining many diverse and lovely forms of life, or whether it risks becoming a dense and suffocating space beneath which only a few rare species might adapt and survive.

In asking such a question, I want to end this paper with an image that has inspired many great works of art in the Catholic tradition.[22] It is the image of the *Mater Misericordiae* which shows Mary as the personification of the maternal Church. In the lovely example known as the *Da Gaeta Mater Misericordiae*, angels hold the hem of the Virgin's cloak and she extends her arms protectively over the People of God. If we look above and beyond the heads of the people gathered there, we see a vast space beneath her cloak

---

[22]It can be found at the following website: http://commons.wikimedia.org/wiki/
File:Da_Gaeta_Mater_Misericordiae.JPG [accessed 12 March 2013].

receding ever further into infinity. That is the space which is open for each and every one of us – God's invitation to come and take our place among all the saints and sinners who are the pilgrim People of God, moving ever forward towards eternity beneath the sheltering canopy of the maternal Church, in which there is always room for more.

9

The Pastoral Strategy of Vatican II: Time for an Adjustment?

Dr Ralph Martin

The pastoral strategy of Vatican II

There is a general consensus among the commentators on Vatican II that a conscious decision was made by John XXIII before the Council, affirmed at the Council itself, to change the pastoral strategy of the Catholic Church in an attempt to communicate more effectively with the modern world and make evangelization more successful. That change was spearheaded by Pope John XXIII when he called for the Council to be pastoral and not issue any condemnations. Pope John XXIII and many others sensed that the Church was becoming increasingly alienated from modern culture and locked into a defensive, apologetic stance that was perceived by the world as negative, condemnatory and unattractive. The Church appeared to many as an archaic institution laden with trappings of an imperial and aristocratic past whose sympathies were with the *ancien regime* of a Church/State symbiosis and far removed from the concerns of the 'modern man'.

Anyone who reads the numerous histories of the Council or theological commentaries on the debates, and then reads the final documents, cannot fail to be impressed by the balance, theological quality, solid scriptural basis, spiritual vitality and pastoral sensitivity of the final texts. They are, indeed, 'compromise' documents, but documents, we believe, that were guided by the Spirit and provide to this day a solid foundation for that true renewal and revitalized evangelization that was the two-fold purpose of the Council. The words of Blessed John Paul II remain true:

> What a treasure there is, dear brothers and sisters, in the guidelines offered to us by the Second Vatican Council. . . . With the passing of the years, the Council documents have lost nothing of their value or brilliance. They need to be read correctly, to be widely known and taken to heart as important and normative texts of the magisterium within the Church's Tradition . . . the great grace bestowed on the Church in the twentieth century: there we find a sure compass by which to take our bearings in the century now beginning.[1]

The Council chose to 'accentuate the positive' in its presentation of the Gospel, highlighting the great beauty of the Trinity, the Incarnation, the ineffable mercy and goodness of God, and the beauty of the Church as a Sacrament of Christ, showing forth his face to the world. It chose to affirm everything it could about the endeavours of the modern world and modern man and not speak much about the consequences of rejecting the good news. As one commentator put it, if this strategy and vision could be successfully presented to the modern world, 'men will storm her doors seeking admission'.[2]

This pastoral strategy has continued to guide the teaching on evangelization and mission in the post-conciliar Church. The reasons given for evangelization in the major post-conciliar documents such as *Evangelii Nuntiandi* (EN) and *Redemptoris Missio* (RM) are predominantly positive, speaking of how Christianity can enrich, or fulfil the human person. Avery Dulles describes this pastoral strategy:

> Neither Vatican II nor the present pope [John Paul II] bases the urgency of missionary proclamation on the peril that the

---

[1] *Novo Millennio Ineunte*, 57.
[2] J. P. Kenny, *Roman Catholicism, Christianity and Anonymous Christianity: The Role of the Christian Today* (Hales Corner, WI: Clergy Book Service, 1973), p. 108.

non-evangelized will incur damnation; rather they stress the self-communicative character of love for Christ, which gives joy and meaning to human existence (RM 10–11; cf. 2 Cor. 5:14).[3]

Richard John Neuhaus studied the reasons given for evangelization in RM and came up with six, none of which speak of the eternal consequences of rejecting the good news, or the fact that those who never hear the good news are not to be presumed saved. He claims that a study of Benedict XVI's writings both as Pope and before would be in harmony with these reasons and this approach as well.[4]

This, of course, is in stark contrast to the traditional focus on the eternal consequences that rest on accepting or rejecting the Gospel that motivated almost 2,000 years of mission. This emphasis also stands in stark contrast to the stress placed on the eternal consequences of accepting or rejecting the Gospel, characteristic of the previous modern papal encyclicals devoted to the missionary task of the Church, published prior to 1960. Pope Benedict XV, on 30 November 1919, promulgated *Maximum Illud* (*On the Propagation of the Catholic Faith throughout the World*). He wrote:

The realization must come as a shock that right now there still remain in the world immense multitudes of people who dwell in darkness and in the shadow of death. According to a recent estimate, the number of non-believers in the world approximates one billion souls. The pitiable lot of this stupendous number of souls is for Us a source of great sorrow. . . . You [speaking to

---

[3] Avery Dulles, 'The Church as Locus of Salvation', in John M. McDermott (ed.), *The Thought of John Paul II: A Collection of Essays and Studies* (Rome: Editrice Pontificia Universita Gregoriana, 1993), p. 176.

[4] John Richard Neuhaus, 'Reviving the Missionary Mandate', in Steven Boguslawski and Ralph Martin (eds), *The New Evangelization: Overcoming the Obstacles* (New York: Paulist, 2008), pp. 34–42. The many very fine pastoral letters published by a number of American bishops in recent years on the New Evangelization mostly follow in the same line; a positive presentation of life in Christ with virtually no mention of the eternal consequences of rejecting the new life. One such example is the very fine 'Pastoral Letter on the New Evangelization' by Archbishop Donald W. Wuerl, *Disciples of the Lord: Sharing the Vision*, published on 23 August 2010, and available on the Archdiocese of Washington, DC website: www.adw.org [accessed 12 March 2013].

missionaries] have been called to carry light to men who lie in the shadow of death and to open the way to heaven for souls that are hurtling to destruction. . . . The sacred obligation of assisting in the conversion of the infidels applies also to them [all Catholics]. . . . Now what class of men is more in need of fraternal help than unbelievers, who live in ignorance of God, and consequently, bound by the chains of their blind and violent desires, are enslaved in the most hideous of all the forms of slavery, the service of Satan?[5]

Pope Pius XI, on 28 February 1926, promulgated *Rerum Ecclesiae – On Catholic Missions*. He stated:

We determined to leave nothing undone which might, by means of apostolic preachers, extend farther and farther the light of the Gospel and make easy for heathen nations the way unto salvation. . . . We ask that there should daily arise to heaven the prayer that the Divine Mercy may descend upon so many unhappy beings, inhabitants of the densely populated pagan countries. . . . Pray that the gift of faith be bestowed upon the almost limitless number of pagans.[6]

Pope Pius XII, on 2 June 1951, promulgated *Evangelii Praecones – On Promotion of Catholic Missions*. He declared:

The Catholic missionary movement both in Christian and pagan lands has gained such force and momentum and is of such proportions as perhaps was never witnessed before in the annals of Catholic missions. . . . It is a great consolation to Us to know that the number of missionary vocations is happily on the increase. . . . When We consider the countless peoples who are to be called to the one fold and to the one haven of salvation by the preaching of these missionaries . . . we pray: There is no God beside thee, O Lord. . . . The object of missionary activity, as all know, is to bring the light of the Gospel to new races and to form new Christians. . . . Pray earnestly for the salvation of the infidel. . . . You are well aware that almost the whole human

---

[5]Pope Benedict XV, *Maximum Illud – On the Propagation of the Catholic Faith Throughout the World*, 30 November 1919; 6, 7, 18, 31.
[6]Pope Pius XI, *Rerum Ecclesiae – On Catholic Missions*, 28 February 1926; 3, 8, 12.

race is today allowing itself to be driven into two opposing camps, for Christ or against Christ. The human race is involved today in a supreme crisis, which will issue in its salvation by Christ, or in its dire destruction.[7]

Pius XII's Encyclical *Fidei Donum* (*On the Present Condition of the Catholic Missions, Especially in Africa*), promulgated on 21 April 1957, conveys a similar concern for the salvation of the unevangelized, 'where some 85,000,000 people still sit in the darkness of idolatry'.[8]

Shortly before Vatican II, on 28 November 1959, Pope John XXIII, to commemorate the 40th anniversary of *Maximum Illud*, issued his own Encyclical on missions, *Princeps Pastorum* (*The Prince of Shepherds, On the Missions, Native Clergy, and Lay Participation*). The emphasis on the urgency of the salvation of souls who are at risk of being eternally lost is considerably diminished but not absent: 'We are everywhere confronted by appeals to Us to ensure the eternal salvation of souls in the best way We can, and a cry seems to reach Our ears: "Help us!" ' (Acts 16:9).[9]

Three of these Encyclicals (*Maximum Illud, Rerum Ecclesia* and *Fidei Donum*) are referenced in a footnote to *Lumen Gentium* 17 (LG) which concludes chapter II of LG with a strong call to evangelization.[10]

An adjustment in pastoral strategy is needed

While there were many sound reasons to emphasize the positive in the Church's relations with the modern world, it has also become clear that an adjustment in her pastoral strategy is needed. Contemporary culture has not stormed 'her doors seeking admission',

---

[7]Pope Pius XII, *Evangelii Praecones – On Promotion of Catholic Missions*, 2 June 1951; 1, 10, 65, 70.

[8]Pope Pius XII, *Fidei Donum – On the Present Condition of the Catholic Missions, Especially in Africa*, 21 April 1957; 20.

[9]Pope John XXIII, *Princeps Pastorum – The Prince of Shepherds, On the Missions, Native Clergy, and Lay Participation*, 18 November 1959; 6.

[10]All five of these pre-1960 mission Encyclicals were referenced in the draft of *De Ecclesia*, AS III/ 1, pp. 191–6.

as one writer we have cited predicted. Contemporary culture has proven more resistant to the Gospel as it has been presented than the Church has been resistant to the secularizing pressures of contemporary culture.

The most important reason for an adjustment in pastoral strategy is that we have a responsibility to transmit revelation as we have received it, in its integrity, proportion and balance. Our goal needs to be to transmit in its entirety the whole teaching of Jesus and the Apostles as it comes to us in scripture, tradition and the authoritative teaching of the Magisterium. Revelation cannot change – although it can be more profoundly understood and expressed – but pastoral strategy can and should change to meet changing circumstances and as the fruits or effectiveness of a particular pastoral strategy can be assessed. Insofar as the Second Vatican Council shaped its message to suit a particular pastoral strategy (radically changing the previous pastoral strategy), it is subject to evaluation and change.

Another important reason to adjust the strategy is that when the eternal consequences that flow from what we choose to believe and how we choose to act are not spoken of for long periods of time, the silence on these dimensions of the Gospel is often taken to mean that they are no longer important, true or relevant.[11]

---

[11]Three books that have addressed these issues in greater depth and have provided a measure of statistical and anecdotal backing for these assertions are: Ralph Martin *Unless the Lord Build the House* (Ave Maria: Notre Dame, 1971); Ralph Martin, *A Crisis of Truth: The Undermining of Faith, Morality and Mission in the Catholic Church* (Servant: Ann Arbor, 1982); Ralph Martin, *The Catholic Church at the End of an Age: What is the Spirit Saying?* (Ignatius: San Francisco, 1994). Avery Dulles, in a foreword to a recent book on evangelization: Timothy E. Byerley, *The Great Commission: Models of Evangelization in American Catholicism* (New York: Paulist Press, 2008), p. ix, cites unsettling statistics, drawn from Nancy T. Ammerman, *Pillars of Faith* (Berkeley: University of California Press, 2005), pp. 117, 134: 'Asked whether spreading the faith was a high priority of their parishes, 75 per cent of conservative Protestant congregations and 57 per cent of African American congregations responded affirmatively, whereas only 6 per cent of Catholic parishes did the same. Asked whether they sponsored local evangelistic activities, 39 per cent of conservative Protestant congregations and 16 per cent of African American congregations responded positively as compared with only 3 per cent of Catholic parishes. Converts to Catholicism often report that on their spiritual journey they received little or no encouragement from Catholic clergy whom they consulted. . . . The Council has often been interpreted as if it had discouraged evangelization'. The Catherine of Siena Institute in Colorado Springs, Colorado, has interviewed tens of thousands of Catholics and their pastors, and makes the point that even among the minority of Catholics who come to Church somewhat

As one commentator has pointed out, when the eternal consequences of believing and obeying or not believing and obeying are
left fuzzy, 'the essential faith of Catholics will then amount to no
more than a vague theism with little specific moral content; just
what it is for a large proportion of Catholics today'.[12]

In this connection, Cardinal Ratzinger spoke of the 'catastrophic
failure of modern catechesis':

The new evangelization we need so urgently today is not to be
attained with cleverly thought out ideas, however cunningly these

---

regularly less than 15 per cent could be considered 'intentional disciples' who have
made Christ the center of their lives, and more probably no more than 5 per cent
(www.siena.org). Cardinal Ratzinger in *The Yes of Jesus Christ*, pp. 39–40, remarked
on the strange phenomenon in conjunction with the collapse of the Church in the
Netherlands after Vatican II. He pointed out that by every statistical measure the
Church in the Netherlands was collapsing and yet, strangely, at the same time an
atmosphere of 'general optimism' was prevalent that seemed to be blind to the actual
situation. 'I thought to myself: what would one say of a businessman whose accounts
were completely in the red but who, instead of recognizing this evil, finding out its
reasons, and courageously taking steps against it, wanted to commend himself to his
creditors solely through optimism? What should one's attitude be to an optimism
that was quite simply opposed to reality?' In my own country, the United States,
the 'official optimism' has been quite strong in the midst of radical decline. When
the American Bishops greeted Pope Benedict XVI on his pastoral visit, they spoke
of our 'vibrant' Church. The statistics from one large American Archdiocese that
are quite typical of the Catholic 'heartland' of the Middle Atlantic, New England,
Mid-Western and Upper Mid-Western States are quite sobering. Just in the 10 year
period of 2000–10, the following happened: infant baptism declined 42.4 per cent;
adult baptisms declined 51.2 per cent; Catholic marriages declined 45.3 per cent;
those seeking full communion with the Church declined 43.6 per cent; household
units that contributed to the annual appeal declined 14.9 per cent and there were
12.8 per cent fewer parishes. While there has been growth in the West, Southwest
and South, a growth which is largely due to Hispanic immigration, not growth
through evangelization, the statistics about the outflow from the Catholic Church
in second and third generation Hispanic Catholic immigrants are not encouraging.
See Edwin Hernández, with Rebecca Burwell and Jeffrey Smith, 'A Study of
Hispanic Catholics: Why Are They Leaving the Catholic Church? Implications for
the New Evangelization', in Steven Boguslawski and Ralph Martin (eds), *The New
Evangelization: Overcoming the Obstacles* (New York: Paulist Press, 2008), pp.
109–41. Shortly before Pope Benedict XVI's visit to the United States, Russell Shaw,
a former spokesman for the American Bishops, in 'Please Look Behind the Bishops'
Potemkin Village' in *The Catholic World Report* (February 2008), pp. 19–22, urged
the American Bishops to stop pretending that everything was fine.
[12]John Lamont, 'What Was Wrong with Vatican II', in *New Blackfriars*, 99, 1013
(January 2007), pp. 92–3. See also John Lamont, 'Why the Second Vatican Council
Was a Good Thing and Is More Important Than Ever', in *New Oxford Review* (July/

are elaborated: the catastrophic failure of modern catechesis is all too obvious. It is only the interaction of a truth conclusive in itself with its proof in the life of this truth that can enable that particular evidence of the faith to be illuminated that the human heart awaits: it is only through this door that the Holy Spirit enters the world.[13]

The popularization of theological theories – which are almost always more nuanced in the scholarly works that propound them – that give the impression that almost everybody is saved, and that perhaps only a few especially evil people end up in hell, and that there are many ways to salvation, has done much to contribute to a 'culture of universalism' not only in Western society as a whole but within the Church as well.[14] In addition, when a 'practical universalism' holds sway in the minds of people, the zeal for holiness and evangelization will certainly be reduced. Both Paul VI and John Paul II bemoaned this lack of zeal and noted the cause for this lack of zeal as often being rooted in false theological theories. Unfortunately, they both stopped short of the full remedy, a full restatement of the Gospel concerning salvation as we find it in Scripture, Tradition and the important sentences of LG 16 which state that even though it is possible under certain very specific conditions for people to be saved without hearing the Gospel, it would be wrong to presume that this is usually the case.

August 2005), pp. 32–6, in which he identifies the positive aspects of Vatican II. For a recent comprehensive study of the religious beliefs of American youth, see Christian Smith with Melinda Lundquist Denton, *Soul Searching: The Religious and Spiritual Lives of American Teenagers* (New York: Oxford University Press, 2005), p. 166, which confirms this judgement, and extends it to the parents of such youth. In this study Catholic youth appeared to be in the worse condition of any Church group as regards orthodox belief. For example 57 per cent of teenage Catholics stated that they maybe or definitely believed in reincarnation. The authors conclude that even though the 'shell' or 'form' of traditional religion is there it has been colonized by an alien spirit which they describe as 'Moralistic Therapeutic Deism.' See also the important study authored by Kenda Creasy Dean, *Almost Christian: What the Faith of Our Teenagers Is Telling the American Church* (New York: Oxford University Press, 2010), especially Chapter 2, 'The Triumph of the Cult of Nice', pp. 25–42.
[13]Ratzinger *The Yes of Jesus Christ*, p. 35.
[14]Unfortunately, some of the remarks of Benedict XVI have furthered this impression, although it appears he may simply be stating theological speculation and not actually teaching in an authoritative way. There are a number of texts that give this impression but the most prominent appearance of this 'supposition' is in the Encyclical *Spe Salvi*. Sections 45–47 of *Spe Salvi* seem to be giving the impression that only a few really evil people are candidates for hell and virtually everybody else will be in purgatory and ultimately heaven.

But very often (*at saepius*), deceived by the Evil One, men have become vain in their reasonings, have exchanged the truth of God for a lie and served the world rather than the Creator (cf. Rom. 1:21, 25). Or else, living and dying in this world without God, they are exposed to ultimate despair. Hence to procure the glory of God and the salvation of all these, the Church, mindful of the Lord's command, 'preach the Gospel to every creature' (Mk. 16:16) takes zealous care to foster the missions [...] (LG 16).

They, for the most part, remained silent on this aspect of the truth, in all probability, in order to remain within the pastoral strategy of Vatican II.[15] Paul VI, after exhorting the Church to keep the missionary impulse alive, says: 'Let us state this fact [the Church's commitment to keep the missionary spirit alive] with joy at a time when there are not lacking those who think and even say that ardour and the apostolic spirit are exhausted, and that the time of the missions is now past'.[16]

As we have previously noted, he clearly identifies the theological currents that are taking away the motivation to evangelize:

Thus one too frequently hears it said, in various terms, that to impose a truth, be it that of the Gospel or to impose a way, be it that of salvation, cannot but be a violation of religious liberty.

---

[15]The Walter Abbott translation that appeared in 1966 translates the Latin phrase *at saepius* as 'but rather often'. The commonly used Flannery translation of the Council documents translates the Latin *at saepius* as 'very often.' This is the translation we are using (Austin Flannery (ed.), *Vatican Council II: The Conciliar and Post Conciliar Documents*, New Revised Edition, vol. I (Northport, NY: Costello Publishing, 1996)). Other English translations use 'but often', (the translation of the National Catholic Welfare Conference, the precursor of the National Council of Catholic Bishops; contained in: *The Sixteen Documents of Vatican II: Introductions by Douglas G. Bushman* (Boston: Pauline Books and Media, 1999)). The Vatican website translation which is available in Appendix I also uses 'but often'. The English translation (by Clarence Gallagher) of *Lumen Gentium* in Norman Tanner's two volume collection of the *Decrees of the Ecumenical Councils* (Washington, DC: Georgetown University Press, 1990) uses 'more often, however'. The French translation of the text that Congar collaborated on translates *at saepius* as 'mais trop souvent'. *L'Église de Vatican II*, Tome I, Texte Latin et Traduction, P.-Th. Camelot (Paris: Cerf, 1966). The Vatican website translation uses 'bien souvent'. The Italian translation on the Vatican website is 'ma molto spesso'. The Spanish translation on the Vatican website is 'pero con mucha frecuencia'.

[16]*EN* 53.

Besides, it is added, why proclaim the Gospel when the whole world is saved by uprightness of heart? We know likewise that the world and history are filled with "seeds of the Word"; is it not therefore an illusion to claim to bring the Gospel where it already exists in the seeds that the Lord Himself has sown? Anyone who takes the trouble to study in the Council's documents the questions upon which these excuses draw too superficially will find quite a different view.[17]

Paul VI responds to the question of the 'imposition of the Gospel' by clarifying that we propose, not impose, disavowing any pressure or coercion, respectful of each person's freedom. His response though to the more serious question of 'why proclaim the Gospel when the whole world is saved by uprightness of heart' leaves one hanging.

God can accomplish this salvation in whomsoever He wishes by ways which He alone knows [he cites AG 7 here]. And yet, if His Son came, it was precisely in order to reveal to us, by His word and by His life, the ordinary paths of salvation. And He has commanded us to transmit this revelation to others with His own authority. It would be useful if every Christian and every evangelizer were to pray about the following thought: men can gain salvation also in other ways, by God's mercy, even though we do not preach the Gospel to them; but as for us, can we gain salvation if through negligence or fear or shame—what St. Paul called "blushing for the Gospel" (Rom. 1:18)—or as a result of false ideas, we fail to preach it?[18]

Paul VI's argument basically comes down to – yes, people can be saved without us evangelizing – but the Lord has asked us to evangelize. There is certainly a force to this argument. But if one simply makes the argument from authority and fails to give the reasons why Christ has asked us to evangelize, then one of the most fundamental reasons of all has not been given, a reason that was the most significant motivation for 2,000 years of heroic evangelization. A primary motivation for the Apostles and the whole history of Christian missions, was knowing from divine revelation

---

[17]EN 80.
[18]Ibid.

that the human race is lost, eternally lost, without Christ, and even though the Church eventually discerned it is possible for people to be saved under certain stringent conditions without explicit faith and baptism, it also clearly recognized that 'very often' this is not actually the case. Therefore it is urgent that the Gospel be preached. Knowing the truth provides the compelling motivation that leads to heroic love in action.

John Paul II also notes the significant negative influence of theological confusion on the will to evangelize. He acknowledges that while the Council intended for there to be a flowering of missionary effort as a fruit of its work, the very opposite has happened, and the Church has seen a waning of missionary fervour since the Council. Despite the many positive fruits of the Council – the Pope explicitly mentions here the emergence of a laity dedicated to evangelization 'which is changing ecclesial life' – there is nevertheless a serious impediment to the full realization of a 'new springtime' which the Pope links to a 'crisis of faith'.

> Nevertheless, in this "new springtime" of Christianity there is an undeniable negative tendency, and the present document is meant to help overcome it. Mission activity specifically directed 'to the nations' (*ad gentes*) appears to be waning, and this tendency is certainly not in line with the directives of the Council and of subsequent statements of the Magisterium.[19]

John Paul II indicates that this should be a concern to all since 'missionary drive has always been a sign of vitality, just as its lessening is a sign of a crisis of faith'.[20] He also hopes by writing this Encyclical 'to clear up doubts and ambiguities regarding missionary activity *ad gentes*'.[21]

Both EN and RM are truly inspiring documents and they provide many eloquently stated reasons for continuing the Church's primary service to the human race, namely, evangelization. However, neither one addresses extensively one of the primary underlying reasons for the waning of mission *ad gentes* or the lack of any significant embrace of the call to a 'new evangelization' or 're-evangelization' (RM 33) of those who perhaps have been baptized but are far from

---

[19]RM 2.
[20]Ibid.
[21]Ibid.

the faith. Neither one elaborates on the Council's main teaching in LG 16 on why 'very often' the possibility of people being saved without hearing the Gospel is not realized.[22]

The need to recover the boldness of apostolic preaching

To present adequately the teaching of LG 16 would entail an unashamed explication of the teaching of Romans about what the human condition actually is apart from Christ. This would include explaining adequately the horror of sin, immorality, idolatry, unbelief; the culpable suppression of the truth; the refusal to worship, thank, and submit; the reality of God's wrath properly understood; and our desperate need for Christ in order for us to be reconciled with God, bringing with it an appropriate fear of the Lord.

As Fr Francis Martin puts it in his study of John's Gospel as it relates to evangelization:

> The essential action of the Paraclete in this passage [Jn 16:7-11] is to prove that the world is culpably wrong, to establish its culpability as *world*. The difficulty arises when we seek to define the recipient of this action. Is it that the world is brought to acknowledge its sin or that the believers are given irrefutable proof that the world is in sin? Basically, it must be the second. If the world were able to acknowledge its sin, it would no longer be the "world," that is, a place which, despite the fact that there is still room for freedom and choice, is nevertheless at its depths a demonic universe of refusal and rejection. . . . The root sin of the world is refusal to believe in Jesus and the place he holds next to

---

[22]Recently, an unpublished text presented by Bishop Thomas Mar Anthonios at a Symposium held at the Pontifical University of Saint Thomas, Rome, 25 March 2011, a document prepared for an upcoming Synod of the Syro-Malankara Church in India, p. 5, cited some of the points we have been making about the need to take into account the complete text of *LG* 16. '*Lumen Gentium* article 16 is often interpreted partially and independently from the rest of the Council teachings on salvation and the "possibility" of salvation is interpreted to mean probability and presumption giving the impression that salvation can be assumed to "people who have never heard the Gospel" and the second part "through no fault of their own" is interpreted lightly and their choice of "exchanging truth for a lie" is often omitted'.

the Father as the Revelation of the Father, the root sin is to reject the Truth. "Whoever believes in the Son has eternal life, whoever disobeys the Son will not see life, but must endure God's wrath" (Jn 3:36).[23]

Fr John Michael McDermott has pointed out that John Paul II was not completely silent on these realities – and treated them to some extent in *Dominum et Vivificantem* – but seldom related them directly to evangelization. Fr McDermott summarizes some of this teaching:

Despite this optimism about the salvation of men expressed in other works, Pope John Paul II surely does not overlook the horrors of sin. . . . Naturally the sinner is the least likely to admit his need for conversion. His sin ties him up in knots of self-justification. The word from without, preached in the Spirit's power, must be met with the workings of the Spirit from within sinful men. The horror of sin and the sinner is hidden from man unless the Spirit teaches him. . . . The universality of human sin is presupposed by the universality of salvation effected by Christ. . . . Hence all men have need of salvation. . . . That insight, of course, led St. Paul (Rom 5:12-21) and the Church to affirm the doctrine of original sin, "the sin that according to the revealed Word of God constitutes the principle and root of all the others." (DV, 33). . . . This turning from truth is mirrored in the rejection of the Word made flesh on Calvary.[24]

---

[23]Francis Martin 'The Spirit of the Lord is Upon Me: The Role of the Holy Spirit in the Work of Evangelization', in Steven Boguslawski and Ralph Martin (eds), *The New Evangelization: Overcoming the Obstacles* (New York: Paulist Press, 2008), pp. 72–3. See also pp. 74–6.

[24]John M. McDermott, 'Reflections on *Dominum et Vivificantem*', in John M. McDermott and John Gavin (eds), *Pope John Paul II on the Body* (Philadelphia: St Joseph's University Press, 2007), pp. 358–9. See also the whole section on the Holy Spirit and sin, pp. 358–64. Fr McDermott 'Universal History and the History of Salvation', in René Latourelle and Rino Fisichella (eds), *Dictionary of Fundamental Theology* (New York: Crossroad, 1994), p. 454, draws the connection between original sin and the need for mission: 'Knowing how difficult it is to live Christ's sacrificial love even with all the helps of the church, recognizing the power of evil that resulted in the Christ's crucifixion and made clear the absolute need for conversion, and having received Christ's explicit command to make disciples of all nations, believers correctly admit that the gospel's emphasis rests upon the necessity of mission'.

Cardinal Joseph Ratzinger also expressed concern about the silence about sin that he thinks has been characteristic of the post-Vatican II era. He recounts a recollection of a conversation he had with a fellow bishop about what would be a suitable theme for a future World Synod of Bishops. The words of Mk 1:15 which record the fundamental theme of Jesus' preaching, concerning the need to believe and repent in light of the coming Kingdom, were being considered as a theme.

> One of the bishops reflected on these words and said that he had the impression that we had long ago actually halved Jesus' message as it is thus summarized. We speak a great deal—and like to speak—about evangelisation and the good news in such a way as to make Christianity attractive to people. But hardly anyone, according to this bishop, dares nowadays to proclaim the prophetic message: Repent! Hardly anyone dares to make to our age this elementary evangelical appeal, with which the Lord wants to induce us to acknowledge our sinfulness, to do penance, and to become other than what we are. Our confrere added that Christian preaching today sounded to him like the recording of a symphony that was missing the initial bars of music, so that the whole symphony was incomplete and its development incomprehensible. With this he touched a weak point of our present-day spiritual situation. Sin has become almost everywhere today one of those subjects that are not spoken about. Religious education of whatever kind does its best to evade it.[25]

The revelation of the power of sin and the need for repentance is a central theme of the entire Bible. The Bible itself sometimes provides some particularly concise summaries of its own teaching on the truth of the human condition and the need for Christ:

> And you he made alive, when you were dead through the trespasses and sins in which you once walked, following the course of this world, following the prince of the power of the air, the spirit that is now at work in the sons of disobedience. Among

---

[25]Joseph Ratzinger, "In the Beginning . . .": A Catholic Understanding of the Story of Creation and the Fall (Grand Rapids: William B. Eerdmans, 1995), pp. 61–2.

these we all once lived in the passions of our flesh, following the desires of body and mind, and so we were by nature children of wrath, like the rest of mankind. But God, who is rich in mercy, out of the great love with which he loved us, even when we were dead through our trespasses, made us alive together with Christ (by grace you have been saved), and raised us up with him, and made us sit with him in the heavenly places in Christ Jesus, that in the coming ages he might show the immeasurable riches of his grace in kindness toward us in Christ Jesus. For by grace you have been saved through faith; and this is not your own doing, it is the gift of God—not because of works, lest any man should boast. For we are his workmanship, created in Christ Jesus for good works, which God prepared beforehand, that we should walk in them (Eph 2:1-10). RSV

The words of Paul to Titus also provide a concise summary:

For we ourselves were once foolish, disobedient, led astray, slaves to various passions and pleasures, passing our days in malice and envy, hated by men and hating one another; but when the goodness and loving kindness of God our Savior appeared, he saved us, not because of deeds done by us in righteousness, but in virtue of his own mercy, by the washing of regeneration and renewal in the Holy Spirit, which he poured out upon us richly through Jesus Christ our Savior, so that we might be justified by his grace and become heirs in hope of eternal life. The saying is sure (Ti 3:3-8) RSV.

Unless we squarely face the bad news – original sin and personal sin have severe consequences – it is impossible really to appreciate the good news (God is rich in mercy, out of the great love with which he loved us we are saved by grace through faith).[26] As one commentator puts it:

The trouble with the Council's approach to mission is that although it stresses that Catholics must seek to convert

---

[26]As one friend put it: 'Before you can preach the Good News, you have to preach the bad news, because if you don't, they'll think that the Good News is not news at all'.

unbelievers, it gives no adequate reason for doing so. It does give Christ's command to evangelize as a reason, but it gives no proper explanation of why that command is given, or of the good that the commandment is supposed to promote. This, of course, means that the command is unlikely to be followed; and it has in fact been largely disregarded since the Council. This lack of an explanation of the reason for evangelization is a departure from Catholic tradition, which has presented evangelization as an activity that should be undertaken in order to save the souls of unbelievers.[27]

An unwise silence should end

Obviously the Council did not intend to depart from the Catholic tradition on this point. The effort to show how the Council is based on Scripture and Tradition contained both within the texts and footnotes of the documents is impressive. An examination of just one of these texts, LG 16, with its footnote references to Thomas Aquinas, Eusebius of Caesarea, and the *Letter of the Holy Office to the Archbishop of Boston*, as well as its explicit citation of Romans 1, demonstrates this. The references in LG 17 to the earlier twentieth century Papal Encyclicals on the urgency of mission in light of the salvation of souls also demonstrates this. There was though perhaps an unwise silence on important elements of scripture and tradition – with the best of intentions. It was a matter of a prudential judgement concerning pastoral strategy. In retrospect it might be fair to say that it was an unwise silence, a flawed pastoral strategy, and we are overdue for a 'rebalancing' of our message and strategy.

It was already apparent to some theologians that there were theological theories circulating which went beyond what the Church understood to be the truth about the salvation of unbelievers that had the potential to undermine evangelization. As early as 1933 astute observations were being made, and substantial articles being written, that showed that theological theories that were beginning to appear which assumed that the mercy of God would not permit many to be lost would convert mission to a matter of 'a greater

---

[27]Lamont, 'What was Wrong with Vatican II', p. 89.

fullness of life' and not really a matter of life or death as regards eternal destiny, and would undermine it. As one such article states, written by a French Dominican theologian:

> If missionary preaching is not so much a question of life or death but rather a question of a greater fullness of life; if it is not a question of life or death for a great number of unbelievers, the Church then is no longer the ordinary way of salvation, but only a school of perfection for great souls called to the fullness of Christian life. The most urgent reason for missions disappears; it will not be equivalently replaced by those reasons that people are trying hard to find, which are not without their value, but until now were only secondary reasons for people to carry out mission.[28]

But these prophetic warnings were not heeded and the tendency was to repeat the argument from authority (we are commanded to evangelize) rather than to elaborate the reasons for the intrinsic necessity of such evangelization; namely, vast numbers of people within and without the Church do not appear to be seeking God and trying to do his will, following the light of their consciences, but are rather exchanging the truth of God for a lie, suppressing the truth, and living in rebellion and immorality and need urgently to be invited to faith and repentance in order to be saved.

It is obvious that the Council itself truly hoped for a great flowering of evangelization but also was aware that there were theories circulating that could undermine this hope. Gérard Philips, the principal drafter of LG, had very strong things to say about the intention of the Council as regards evangelization. While God is at

---

[28]Étienne Hugueny, 'Le scandale édifiant d'une exposition missionnaire', in *Revue Thomiste*, 76 (1933), pp. 217–42, and 78–9 (1933), pp. 533–67. The article appeared in two parts and the above citation is from pp. 227–8, of the first part. ('*Si la prédication missionnaire n'est pas tant une question de vie ou de mort qu'une question de plénitude de vie; si elle n'est pas une question de vie ou de mort pour un grand nombre d'infidèles, l'Église n'est plus la voie normale du salut, mais seulement une école de perfection pour les grandes âmes appelées à la plénitude de la vie chrétienne. La raison la plus urgente des missions disparait ; elle ne sera pas équivalemment remplacée par toutes celles qu'on s'efforcera de trouver, qui ne sont pas sans valeur, mais qui jusqu'ici n'étaient que des motifs complémentaires pour tous les missionnaires.*')

work in the authentic elements of truth to be found in the world's religions and even in atheists, nevertheless, he repeatedly states, we have an obligation to evangelize since we have been commanded by Christ to do so, noting the citation of Mk 16: 15 in the actual text. He even says that failure to obey the command to preach the Gospel would actually be a form of 'blasphemy'.[29]

And then, aware of theological undercurrents already undermining evangelization, already discouraging missionaries, Philips emphatically denies that there is any basis in LG for this to happen:

> We cannot remain silent on a paradoxical situation, stirred up by a misunderstanding of the doctrine of the Council. Under the influence of an extension of conciliar perspectives, the missionary zeal of some has been weakened. No ecclesial document has ever emphasized with such insistence the universal missionary obligation as *Lumen Gentium* did, not only in this text, but throughout the Constitution, from the first to the last page. True missionary zeal is the fruit of a pure faith and unselfish charity: that is what Vatican II aimed at, not indifference.[30]

Philips, of course, is right, but the section of LG 16 – the last three sentences – that could have forestalled such theological misadventures, and which grounded the Council's teaching on this point in scripture and tradition, has been virtually ignored. LG 17 forms the conclusion of the related series of sections (13–17) and gives a stirring call to evangelization, obviously based on the truth that despite the 'ordering' of the non-Christian religions, and indeed of all humanity towards Christ and the Church, that in itself does

---

[29]Philips, *L'Église*, p. 210. 'Our free adherence to the will of God imposes on us the duty of preaching the Gospel; the failure to do so makes us culpable of a form of blasphemy'. ('*Notre libre adhésion à la volonté de Dieu nous impose le devoir de prêcher l'Evangile, faute de quoi nous nous rendons coupables d'une espèce de blasphème*'.)

[30]Ibid., p. 219 ('Nous ne pouvons passer sous silence une situation paradoxale, suscitée par une méprise sur la doctrine du Concile. Sous l'influence de l'extension des perspectives *conciliaires, il en est chez qui le zèle missionnaire s'est affaibli. Et pourtant jamais document ecclésiastique n'a souligné avec autant d'insistance le devoir missionnaire universel que Lumen Gentium, non seulement à cet endroit mais à travers toute la Constitution, de la première à la dernière page. Le vrai zèle missionnaire est le fruit de la foi pure et de la charité désintéressée : c'est cela que vise Vatican II et non l'indifférence*'.)

not imply salvation.[31] Salvation requires a response to grace, which is most likely to happen in response to the preaching of the Gospel. LG 16 concluded by citing the 'great commission' that Jesus gives his disciples to evangelize in Mk 16:16. LG 17 cites the other 'great commission' from Mt 28: 18-20.

> The Church has received this solemn command of Christ from the Apostles and she must fulfill it to the very ends of the earth (cf. Acts 1:8). Therefore she makes the words of the apostle her own, "Woe to me if I do not preach the Gospel" (1 Cor. 9:16), and accordingly never ceases to send heralds of the Gospel. . . . By her proclamation of the Gospel, she draws her hearers to receive and profess the faith, she prepares them for baptism, snatches them from the slavery of error, and she incorporates them into Christ so that in love for him they grow to full maturity . . . [to] the confusion of the devil, and the happiness of man. Each disciple of Christ has the obligation of spreading the faith to the best of his ability (LG 17).

Perhaps the reason why these strong calls to evangelization, which do, in a secondary way, mention elements of the 'biblical world view' concerning sin, error and the work of the devil, were not able to counter successfully the undermining theological currents is that the argument from authority is not a strong enough argument for ordinary human beings. The reasons for the command – namely,

---

[31]Kenny, *Roman Catholicism*, pp. 88–9, provides a very sympathetic account of Rahner's theory of the anonymous Christian, but notes the serious difficulties of a one-sided positive assessment of the non-Christians religions. 'History unfolds a long and grim tally of craven fears and terrors, hag-ridden superstitions and inhibitions, taboos, sorcery, human sacrifice and sacred prostitution springing from or cloaked over with the name of religion. . . . Always, even in their most lofty representatives, non-Christian religions are stricken with ambiguity. On the one-hand they are embraced, upheld and penetrated by the compassionate love of the unknown Father whom they seek in shadows and images. On the other, they are enmeshed in the web of man's pride and selfishness. Whatever truth they stand for comes from the Spirit of truth, but it needs constantly to be disengaged from false, excessive, depraved accretions. The yearning for God that they voice tends to get stifled or muted by a denial or turning aside from God. Hope impels them to reach out for God's hand, but self-reliance pushes them to have recourse to human devices and techniques of salvation. They want to adore God but not uncommonly they end up by idolatrously manipulating him'.

that the eternal destinies of human beings are really at stake and for many people the preaching of the Gospel can make a life or death, heaven or hell, difference – need to be unashamedly stated. This is certainly why Jesus often spoke of the eternal consequences of not accepting his teaching – being lost forever, hell – and did not just give the command to evangelize. This is why Mk 16:16, which is referenced in LG 16 but not directly quoted, makes explicit that what is at stake is being 'saved' or 'condemned'. Jesus makes clear that Christianity is not a game or an optional enrichment opportunity but a precious and urgent opportunity to find salvation and escape damnation. In fidelity to the teaching of Christ this is what motivated 2,000 years of heroic missionary work and the heroic witness of countless martyrs.

Fr Francis Sullivan, in his account of the history of the development of doctrine, draws our attention to the moving prayer of St Francis Xavier which he prayed before receiving communion:

> Everlasting God, Creator of all things, remember that you alone have created the souls of infidels, whom you have made to your image and likeness. Behold, O Lord, how hell is being filled with them to your dishonor.[32]

Fr Sullivan suggests that Xavier prayed this prayer not because they were condemned to hell due to original sin, but because of their personal sins of idolatry and vice.

> The pathos of this prayer can well be explained by the fact that Xavier believed, with St. Paul (cr. Rom. 1:18-32), that people would be justly condemned for sins of idolatry and vice. He had seen enough of these in his missionary work to be pessimistic about the chances that many pagans had escaped condemnation to hell. His urgency about preaching the Gospel was heightened by his experience that only through the acceptance of Christian faith and the grace of the sacraments were people cured of their tendencies to idolatry and vice.[33]

---

[32] Georg Shurhammer, *Francis Xavier, His Life, His Times,* trans. M. Joseph Costelloe, vol. 4 (Rome: The Jesuit Historical Institute, 1982), pp. 505–6. Cited by Francis Sullivan, *Salvation Outside of the Church? Tracing the History of the Catholic Response* (Eugene, OR: Wipf and Stock, 2002), p. 86.
[33] Sullivan, p. 86.

Ratzinger's analysis of *Schema 13*, which became the Pastoral Constitution on the Church in the Modern World, *Gaudium et Spes* (GS), makes some similar points.

The chief concern of the text was to speak to contemporary man; thus it had tried to express fundamental theological ideas in a modern way, and in doing so got even further away from scriptural language than did its scholastic predecessors. Biblical citations were little more than ornamental. . . . What interest could an outsider find in a theological statement which had largely divorced itself from its own origins?[34]

Norman Tanner provides a good account of the debate on the multiple drafts of *Schema 13* and notes that concerns like Ratzinger's were often raised.

There was also the question of whether the decree was indulging in superficial humanism and naïve optimism about the human state and being insufficiently attentive to evil and the reality of sin.[35]

Tanner's judgement is that there is sufficient balance in the actual document regarding the reality of sin, but 'maybe after the council the pendulum swung to the other extreme'.[36] Tanner also notes that when using certain key concepts such as 'signs of the times' and 'the world', GS was not using them in the way they are used in

---

[34]Joseph Ratzinger, *Theological Highlights of Vatican II*, trans. Henry Traub, Gerard C. Thormann and Werner Barzel (New York: Paulist Press, 1966), p. 153. Avery Dulles, 'Pope Benedict XVI: Interpreter of Vatican II', in Avery Dulles (ed.), *Church and Society: The Lawrence J. McGinley Lectures, 1988-2007* (New York: Fordham University Press, 2008), p. 480, has done a study of the commentaries that Ratzinger has done on Vatican II, from the early work right during and after the Council up until that of his papacy. While there have been some shifts in evaluation, Dulles concludes: 'Notwithstanding the changes, Benedict XVI has shown a fundamental consistency'. Cardinal Ratzinger, *Principles of Catholic Theology: Building Stones for a Fundamental Theology*, trans. Sr. Mary Francis McCarthy (San Francisco: Ignatius Press, 1987), pp. 378–93, also provides a detailed and very helpful evaluation of the final document, and its subsequent reception.
[35]Norman Tanner, *The Church and the World: Gaudium et Spes, Inter Mirifica* (New York: Paulist Press, 2005), p. 9.
[36]Ibid., p. 68.

the Bible, but in a contemporary, secular manner, which inevitably led away from a spiritually discerning, biblically based approach to contemporary culture.[37]

Even Karl Rahner, who participated in drafting GS, later had reservations.

> Although I took part in the elaboration of *Gaudium et Spes* at the Council I would not deny that its undertone is too euphoric in its evaluation of humanity and the human condition. What it says may be true, but it produces the overall impression that it is enough to observe its [GS's] norms, and everything will more or less turn out well.[38]

In one of his later interviews, Rahner bluntly admitted the document's weaknesses.

> So the Council's decree *Gaudium et Spes* can be blamed, despite all that is right in it, for underestimating sin, the social consequences of human guilt, the horrible possibilities of running into historical dead-ends, and so on.[39]

Ratzinger applauds the document for its effort to move away from what had been the only two kinds of doctrinal pronouncements in the Church's history – 'the creed of obligation and the anathema of negation'.

Both kinds of pronouncement made sense only within the realm of faith; they were based on faith's claim to authority. Since the beginning of the modern era there had been increasingly smaller circles of people ready to bow to the authority of the teaching Church.

Yet, he wished that the substitutes – authoritative pronouncements now based on natural law as interpreted by the Church,

---

[37]Ibid., pp. 41 and 49.

[38]Karl Rahner, 'Christian Pessimism', in *Theological Investigations*, vol. 22 of 23, trans. Joseph Doncell (New York: The Crossroad Publishing Company, 1991), pp. 155–62.

[39]Karl Rahner, Paul Imhof and Hubert Biallowons (eds), *Faith in a Wintry Season: Conversations and Interviews with Karl Rahner in the Last Years of His Life*, trans. Harvey D. Egan (New York: Crossroad, 1990), p. 125.

and dialogue – had included a clear option for 'the proclamation of the Gospel, thus opening up the faith to the non-believer and abdicating all claim to authority other than the intrinsic authority of God's truth, manifesting itself to the hearer of the message'.[40]

Ratzinger clearly holds that the inspired assertions of the sacred authors of Scripture are indeed God's Word and should be proclaimed with authority and received as authoritative. He draws our attention to the fact that only Jesus sees the Father and the things of the Father, and it is only in our own union with Jesus and our attentive reception of His Word that we, too, can see, by faith and by the Spirit's gifts of wisdom, knowledge and understanding, what is true.

> In its innermost essence, the Christian faith is a participation in this act whereby Jesus *sees*. His act of seeing makes possible his word, which is the authentic expression of what he sees. Accordingly, what Jesus sees is the point of reference for our faith, the specific place where it is anchored. [41]

He also spelt out more explicitly the deficiencies he saw in the document.

> Despite all disavowals, [the document exhibits] an almost naïve progressivist optimism which seemed unaware of the ambivalence of all external human progress.... Most important, the schema as a whole tended, in its definition of the relationship between the Christian and the technological world, to see the real meaning of the Christological in the sacred aura it confers upon technological achievement.... [This is] a horrible perversion of Christianity.... The schema speaks of the victories of mankind, and means by this the phases of technological progress. The Scriptures also know the language of victory but what they mean is the victory of faith, of love . . . the great victory of Jesus Christ . . . . The world is not redeemed by machinery but by love.[42]

---

[40]Ratzinger, *Theological Highlights*, pp. 156–7.
[41]Joseph Ratzinger, *Christianity and the Crisis of Cultures*, trans. Brian McNeil (San Francisco: Ignatius Press, 2006), pp. 104–5.
[42]Ibid., pp. 158–9.

He applies the biblical world view that is embodied in the opening chapters of Romans to the issues raised by GS:

> We recognize that the small righteousness we manage to build up in ourselves is nothing but an emergency morality in the midst of our radical unrighteousness. We are directly and forcefully reminded of St. Paul when we find ourselves forced from behind our shell of protective speculation, forced to admit that our righteousness is nothing but a temporary expedient in the midst of unrighteousness. We find ourselves crying for mercy to him who makes just the unjust. . . . The foremost intention of the Council was to reveal this need for Christ in the depth of the human heart so as to make man able to hear Christ's call.[43]

When Ratzinger commented on some of the theories that were undermining evangelization in connection with *Ad Gentes* (AG), he made a significant statement, which deserves to be noted. He comments on theological theories that saw the world religions as salvific.

> Here, again, closer reflection will once more demonstrate that not all the ideas characteristic of modern theology are derived from Scripture. This idea is, if anything, alien to the biblical-thought world or even antipathetic to its spirit. The prevailing optimism, which understands the world religions as in some way salvific agencies, is simply irreconcilable with the biblical assessment of these religions.[44]

---

[43]Ibid., p. 171.

[44]Ibid., p. 173. Thomas O'Meara in 'Yves Congar: Theologian of Grace in a Wide World', in Gabriel Flynn (ed.), *Yves Congar: Theologian of the Church* (Louvain/ Grand Rapids: Peter's Press/W.B. Eerdmans, 2005), p. 385, generally sympathizes with Congar's views on the salvation of those who have not heard the gospel, but comments: 'In the 1960s, Congar's evaluation of non-Christian or non-Biblical religions followed by billions of the world's inhabitants remains somewhat negative because unfashionably he would not overlook aspects of religions that are destructive, false, or idolatrous'. O'Meara is not pleased with Congar's conservatism on this matter: 'He sometimes too easily accepts the dichotomy offered by those holding that if you do not have a strong evangelization of an evil world you have no advocacy of the Gospel and no reason for missions'. He cites pp. 211–21 of Congar's essay commenting on sections 2 to 9 of *Ad Gentes*, Yves Congar 'Principes Doctrinaux', in *L'Activité missionnaire de l'Église* (Paris: Editions du Cerf, 1967)

It is a commonplace to state that Scripture is the soul of theology, but it is easy enough to drift into speculation that eventually departs from both the letter and spirit of Scripture or to adopt a pastoral strategy that does so. Ratzinger's reference to the 'biblical-thought world' and its 'spirit' are important to note. The profound analysis of the fully culpable 'suppression of the truth' which is described in Romans 1 with the subsequent downward personal and social spiral needs to be recovered to understand the situation we are facing today. We have not seen that 'biblical thought world' or its 'spirit' adequately 'handed on' in the post-conciliar years. This omission needs to be corrected if the urgent call for a new evangelization is to achieve its considerable promise in the traditionally Christian nations who are now in massive apostasy and in the re-energizing of primary evangelization to the unevangelized peoples of the world.[45]

As Cardinal Ratzinger reminds us, the renewal of the Church and the true implementation of Vatican II, is not a matter of a 'reform of the Church by paper', or a 'paper-dominated Christianity', but rather a matter of a deeper 'yes' to the call to conversion and holiness and the embodiment in living witnesses of the hope and promise of Christ and the Council.

Whether or not the Council becomes a positive force in the history of the Church depends only indirectly on texts and

---

as evidence of Congar's views. Jerome P. Theisen, *The Ultimate Church and the Promise of Salvation* (Collegeville: St John's University Press, 1976), pp. 65–81, reviews all of Congar's writings that touch on the subject of the theological axiom *Extra ecclesia nulla salus*.

[45] As John Paul II stated in *Novo Millennio Ineunte*, 40: 'Even in countries evangelized many centuries ago, the reality of a 'Christian society' which, amid all the frailties which have always marked human life, measured itself explicitly on Gospel values, is now gone.' Norman Tanner, *The Church and the World*, pp. 83–4 and 87–9, uncharacteristically, speaks rather dramatically of the obvious decline of Christianity in Western Europe and North America since the Council: 'The wave of immigrants seeking entry into Europe, as well as the marked decline in the birthrate in many parts of this continent, furnish obvious parallels with the decline and fall of the Roman Empire in the fourth and fifth centuries CE. . . . It may well be, indeed, that the Catholic Church in the twenty-first century is heading toward another Babylonian captivity. Diminished and shackled in Europe, its principal home for many centuries, it may live as an exile in much of the rest of the world, harassed and threatened'. Tanner thinks that GS may in this case help us deal with the diverse, pluralistic, situations that we will encounter.

organizations; the crucial question is whether there are individuals—saints—who, by their personal willingness, which cannot be forced, are ready to effect something new and living. The ultimate decision about the historical significance of Vatican Council II depends on whether or not there are individuals prepared to experience in themselves the drama of the separation of the wheat from the cockle and thus to give to the whole a singleness of meaning that it cannot gain from words alone.[46]

Pastoral application

But, one may ask, how can the biblical world view really be preached today to a culture that is so resistant, indeed, hostile to any talk of eternal consequences for unrepented sin? I would suggest one simple but profound text from John's Gospel as a possible model. The text is very familiar but it is often not very closely read or explicated: 'For God so loved the world that he gave his only begotten Son, that whoever believes in him should not perish but have eternal life' (Jn 3:16).

It's important to emphasize in any preaching of the Gospel – this 'Good News' – that this proclamation is all about love. It begins with God's love for the world, it continues with God's love for the world and it ends with God's love for the world. It's also important to point out that this love is concretely focused and made available to us in the person of his Son. God's love is made accessible in the person of Jesus. Even though we may be tempted to think that this is too narrow or not fair, the fact is that this is reality, this is where God's love can be found and responded to, and we ignore this reality at our great peril.

It is then important to emphasize that the way this love, mercy, forgiveness comes to us personally is through our faith in this provision of God for our salvation, his Son and his saving deeds (incarnation, cross, resurrection, ascension, return in Glory). A response of faith, implying repentance and surrender, is essential. Mercy, forgiveness, salvation isn't automatic. It is a distorted understanding of Divine Mercy to presume that it is automatically

---

[46]Ratzinger, *Principles of Catholic Theology*, pp. 375 and 377.

applied to human beings with no response on their part. Even St Faustina, the Apostle of Divine Mercy, records in her diary the journey through hell that she was taken on so that, as she reported the Lord to have told her, that no one can say that there is no hell and that there is no one there.[47] It is also important to explain in a loving but clear way that if we refuse to believe and repent we are placing ourselves on the broad way that leads to destruction; we are at great risk of 'perishing'.

Of course any communication of the Gospel needs to be sensitive to the person(s) who are being addressed, the leading of the Holy Spirit, and what would be the most helpful communication right now to help them on their way. Everything doesn't have to be said at once, but eventually, every element must be said. Any preaching of the Gospel whether in personal conversations, in structured religious education programs or other teaching situations, or in liturgical preaching, is not faithful to the message we have been entrusted with handing on, if out of a false understanding of compassion, we don't tell people the whole truth.

---

[47]*Diary*, p. 741; see also p. 1396.

10

Interviewed by Gavin D'Costa

Cardinal Godfried Danneels

This conversation between Cardinal Danneels and Gavin D'Costa took place on Wednesday, 17 October 2012 at Clifton Cathedral, Bristol. The Cardinal visited the diocese to give the final talk for its Vatican II lecture series.

D'Costa: It's a great privilege to talk with you Cardinal Danneels, I am Gavin D'Costa and I teach at the University and I want to speak to you about your experience of Vatican II. Can you tell us your first memories of the Council?

Danneels: I didn't participate in the Council but I had conversations with the Bishop of Bruges at the time who was there. We had several conversations during the intersession. I was a priest and professor at a major seminary in Bruges. I remember that of everything that happened in the Council and of all that was decided, everything was already growing in many parts of Europe and in our own country before the Council and it didn't come out of the blue. For example, almost everything that you can find in Sacrosanctum Concilium was already practiced here and in other countries before the announcement of the Council. Also, the new exegetical methods that were accepted were taught in the major seminaries by the professors in Bruges, for example.

D'Costa: So you could say that the Council was catching up with certain parts of Europe, like Belgium?

Danneels: Yes. Also we knew that there was a problem with the revolution that took place during the Council that we could not see and of which we were afraid. The professors of the seminary were concerned that all those 2,500 bishops had been formed with the classical theological methods found in the manuals, neo-Scholasticism. We were worried that they would reproduce these old formulas and not engage with more modern challenges, theologically speaking.

D'Costa: Would you say that for your church in Belgium after the Council, the changes that happened were not that significant because they'd already been happening?

Danneels: The changes were not that great in the minds of professors and theologians but were greater for the lay Catholics who didn't know anything about all of the discussions that had been going on for the theologians in Europe. And of course, the vernacular in the liturgy had a deep, deep influence on people that they didn't expect.

D'Costa: We often hear that there was a kind of tension between 'the majority' and 'the minority' at the Council, the more liberal majority and the more conservative minority. What was your sense of that difference during the intersession when people were reporting back to you as a young priest?

Danneels: I think these tensions had been difficult, the majority against the minority, as there had been some very controversial and big questions being discussed. For example, on the religious freedom as taught in Dignitats Humanae and in Nostra Aetate – the document on the Jews as well as the relation of the Church to other non-Christian religions. These two documents really highlighted differences. The issue about the vernacular in the liturgy was not so contested, but then again there was still a type of difference there. All this was discussed. There was a small minority that was very strong in affirming the classical themes and the classical decisions that occasionally caused tensions. You can read of all this very easily in the diaries of the experts – Yves Congar and Henri de Lubac for example – and you can see that there were serious discussions and tensions.[1]

D'Costa: Do you think that those tensions were reconciled in the sense that all of the documents were constantly reworded and voted on so as to get a large majority in support? Lumen Gentium actually had Pope Paul VI intervening in order to make sure that

---

[1]See, for example: Yves Congar, *My Journal of the Council*, trans. Mary John Ronayne and Mary Cecily Boulding (Adelaide: ATF Theology, 2012) and Henri de Lubac, *Carnets du Concile* (Paris: Cerf, 2007). Two volumes.

the minority's concerns were being met. Do you feel that it was a victory for both groups at the end or a victory of one over the other?

Danneels: No it was not a victory of one over the other because the documents were composed with a fine sense of the necessary balance between different opinions. Lumen Gentium was written by Professor Philips.[2] He was a Belgian and he had the art of composing by taking different elements and welding them into a text where each group could find his own opinion or feeling. And the final votes were in favour of nearly all the documents of the Council, except for the most difficult vote for the document on religious freedom. However, that was still ultimately passed.

D'Costa: Many of the changes that happened after the Council, in the name of the Council, about liturgy are contested today. Some argue that many of the changes that took place in local and national churches and were not actually sanctioned by the Council documents.

Danneels: There have been exaggerations, certainly, since the Council. The progress afterwards has from time to time not been good. In some countries, people went much too far, but for the moment many of those problems have been dealt with. There are still some places where people were so progressive in the hope was that they would draw more people in into the churches because of the changes of liturgy – and it has been exactly the contrary. Nobody believes that these wild experimental things will do good to the Church. I think that some of it has been about wild experimentation rather than true progress. But this is always inevitable after a Council.

D'Costa: Some critics, mainly the conservative critics, argue that the changes in the liturgy resulted in the emptying of the churches in Europe. Do you think that is a gross exaggeration?

Danneels: Some people, very few, think that. However, the reason for the absence of people in the churches is not the liturgy, not the vernacular or the non-vernacular, not the Latin or the non-Latin, but rather it is the cultural climate and evolution of indifference. What we change and what we conserve has little influence on the development of the religious consciousness of the people. It's too easy to say that all of those things are the fruit, the negative fruit, of

---

[2]Msgr. Gérard Philips (1899–1972), Louvain theologian.

the Council. I ask instead: what would it have been like if there had been no Council? It would have been worse.

D'Costa: There is another other aspect of the Council which was very important for many Catholics. After Vatican I we have a theme which Vatican II emphasized and developed: the papal role. In Lumen Gentium we get the development of the notion of collegiality as complementing what Vatican I said about papal authority. Some Catholics feel that collegiality has never really been developed after the Council in the way that Vatican II had wanted it to be developed. You played a key role in the 1985 Synod which addressed this.[3] What is your view about the exercising of collegiality in the church?

Danneels: It was decided at Vatican II that there should be collegiality. We bishops have to go to Rome to a synod, for example, and there are very good relations between the bishops. There are the Episcopal Conferences, the Bishops Conferences, but they are not deliberative. They are consultative. I think that we are still looking for how a way to translate collegiality in juridical terms. It will not be easy to do this: to make a working balance between the primacy of the pope and the collegiality of the bishops, there will always be tensions. In the course of the history of the church we have always found these tensions. I think we will not be able to move away from these tensions until Christ's return at the end of the world! It is like that for many issues in the Christian faith: for example, there is grace and there is my free will. How can the two live together? But they do. Christ is God and He is Man, how can that fit? There is primacy and there is collegiality of the bishops. There is grace and there is ascetic effort. These are the famous paradoxes of the Christian faith and we must not imagine they get resolved easily.

D'Costa: If Pope Benedict asked you to give him advice about what specific juridical mechanism could be put into place to help try and capture some of what is required, what would you yourself suggest?

Danneels: I would suggest that there should be what they call in French, a *conseil de la couronne*. A kind of senate of five, six or seven

---

[3] 1985 Extraordinary Synod convened on 24 November 1985. Final report can be found at: http://www.ewtn.com/library/CURIA/SYNFINAL.HTM [accessed 12 March 2013].

people, bishops and cardinals, and have them all over the world where, for a period of 4 or 5 years, they form consultative groups to the Pope. With such groups, the Pope can speak what he is thinking, not in the view of taking decisions. These groups could voice every need felt by the different continents to the Pope without pressing and pushing him and calling for action. Normally, the Curia should do this. But I think when you are in Rome, you become Roman! That's irresistible. And the Roman Curia is in Rome.

D'Costa: But the Curia right now is at its most international in its composition? What do you mean?

Danneels: Admittedly, the Curia is better than it ever has been, but the Roman spirit is everywhere. It is irresistible, and it is not at all false or bad, but I think that there must be more echoes heard from the whole world and not only from the mind of the Curia.

D'Costa: So you suggest groups, but not with any juridical powers?

Danneels: No, just free speech. A freedom of speech is most important and for the Pope to hear these groups.

D'Costa: Do you think that does not take place at the Synods?

Danneels: No, in a Synod there are 250 Bishops and it is very difficult to have a developed and complex debate. You can say something to the Pope who is there and who listens, but that is not the same thing as a group of good meaning people who are there to help the Pope, not to influence him but to help him and ensure that he is correctly informed. These groups would hold meetings every three months or something like that. Because it's not juridical, there's no decision-making, it's rather bringing out the importance of the freedom of speech and the exchange of frank views.

D'Costa: We should send a copy of your idea to Pope Benedict.

Danneels: He already knows it.

D'Costa: Another major theme of the Council was ecumenism. This was very strong in some parts of Europe. In England, of course, it has been a major area with the Anglican Communion. To summarize: before the Council, other Christian groups were seen as not having a proper status and there was not an official dialogue with them. After the Council, some have characterized the shift in this way: that the true Church subsists in the Catholic Church and the other Christian churches have elements of truth in them, but finally, there must be a unity under the Pope. An Anglican friend of mine said this is really not that different from before, you Catholics are simply saying to us that you must in the end accept the Pope's jurisdiction and then we can have unity. But for us as Anglicans, he said, unity is accepting genuine Christian differences. What are your thoughts on this?

Danneels: There are differences and there are differences. I think that Peter is the *primus* of the church of Jesus. It is difficult to deny this because it is in the Gospel. It is another thing to say that the Pope has jurisdiction over every man and every people as it has been defined in Vatican I. I think that is not a proper understanding of jurisdiction. Jurisdiction over every Roman Catholic; yes that is right. But I think that Archbishop Rowan Williams and certainly his predecessor Archbishop George Carey are convinced that there must be a Petrine function, a Petrine charisma in the church, but how to do it concretely is another question. In that sense I cannot accept that the primacy of the Pope has to disappear to make unity for the unity has to be made and signified in some way. From time to time there are opinions voiced in the Anglican church that say to have a Pope is not completely negative because it's very difficult to conserve the union and the unity when there is no central authority and no visible sign of unity. However, how much juridical power needs to be given to this authority is again another question and very complex.

D'Costa: Both John Paul II and Cardinal Ratzinger, when he was a Cardinal, were emphasizing that it was possible to have the emphasis on primacy and that the level of jurisdiction was something that could be worked out together and over a long term.

Danneels: It has been worked out during the history of the church in different senses but always there was the primacy of Peter. The way to put it into practice has been different throughout that history and it was very different in the first centuries compared to the nineteenth and twentieth centuries'.

D'Costa: Can I turn to another topic which is the question of other religions? Many people were profoundly happy that suddenly not only other Christians but Jews, Muslims, Hindus and Buddhists were acknowledged in Lumen Gentium and Nostra Aetate. One big debate that has happened since the Council, and this is related to Father Jacques Dupuis very specifically, was: did the Council on some level legitimate other religions as means to salvation? This has been a topic that has been greatly debated. Many Catholic theologians argue this can be found in the implications of the Council's teachings. What is your view?

Danneels: First, you have to distinguish between the Jews, the Muslims, the Hindus and the Buddhists. The Jews are our ancestors, so that's a unique relationship, and also Islam comes from Moses and Mohammed. I think that the classical doctrine that there are elements of truth in Buddhism and Hinduism is completely acceptable. There are some things which are more developed in those non-theistic kinds of religions than in Europe: for example with their emphasis on interiority and their techniques of meditation. Catholicism does not have those techniques. Catholics have other practices, yes, but not those. So there is much to be learnt and much need for dialogue.

D'Costa: I know lots of young Catholics who go to Buddhism in order to learn about meditation and yet remain Catholics. Do you think this type of learning is a healthy and good thing?

Danneels: As long as these are techniques that have no special meaning, then techniques are techniques. You can go and look for them in different ways and this does not make you a renegade. However, you must be careful. The technique is always, to some extent, founded in convictions and in a kind of faith, and that is more difficult for it can involve the implicit acceptance of beliefs that might be contrary to Catholicism. But normally technique is just technique.

D'Costa: In 2005 Pope Benedict gave his famous speech to the Curia about how to interpret Vatican II and the theme was continuity and reform. How would you explain this debate to non-theologians who don't really know what this is all about.

Danneels: I think that there are revolutions in Catholic teaching but revolutions are not ruptures. There is continuity and discontinuity at the same time. There is a continuation of the tradition that is evident; yet, there are revolutions and discontinuities of practice as we apply that tradition to new questions. There is therefore an evolution going on which is organic and does not interrupt the tradition and is not against it. This is how the development of doctrine happens. But to see fully the organic evolution we have to wait a long time because these processes take hundreds of years to settle and of course we need a certain critical distance. The culture in which we are living and the thoughts of that culture also bring with them insights that deepen the Church's understanding of the world.

D'Costa: Thank you for your reflections.

INDEX